The WAY
the TRUTH
and the LIFE

THE SAVIOUR

"I am the way, the truth, and the life."—John 14:6.

The WAY the TRUTH and the LIFE

RALPH PALLEN COLEMAN'S
Paintings of the Old and New Testaments
Reproduced in Color

With Interpretations by
ELIZABETH MORTON
in Collaboration with the Artist

THE JOHN C. WINSTON COMPANY
Philadelphia • Toronto

INTRODUCTION ➣ ➣ ➣ ➣ ➣

A generation or more ago it was the custom in many families for all of the members to sit in a group around the fireplace on Sunday afternoon to listen to readings from the family Bible. Usually that large Bible contained brightly lithographed pictures of Biblical heroes, places, and events. To the younger members of the family the pictures were an exciting part of the afternoon program.

Those hours of shared pleasure are a rarity today, for unfortunately the growing tendency of the present generation is for each individual member to pursue his own interests independently of the others.

Perhaps one reason for this lack of companionship is that not too many current books can be shared by parents and growing members of the family.

The publishers, in presenting this beautiful collection of religious paintings by Ralph Pallen Coleman, have purposely designed THE WAY, THE TRUTH, AND THE LIFE so that the book may be enjoyed by children and adults alike.

In the paintings the reader will find a pictorial history of the Bible; in the text he will find a descriptive interpretation of each painting, introducing young and old to the great literary, historical, and religious treasures of the Bible.

"Thy word is a lamp unto my feet, and a light unto my path."—
Ps. 119:105.

Philadelphia
1958

The Old Testament

NOAH'S SACRIFICE ❧ ❧ ❧ ❧ ❧ ❧

WHEN the waters of the Flood ceased, the ark came to rest on the mountain range of Ararat in Armenia on a peak nearly 17,000 feet above sea level.

Then God told Noah to send out all the living creatures, and for him and his wife and his sons and their wives to follow.

Noah's first act after leaving the ark was to build an altar and to offer a sacrifice to the God of his redemption.

The altar was made of stones, built in pyramidal form and set up on the rocks close by the ark. The sacrifice was presumably an animal one, for the Bible states that Noah "took of every clean beast, and of every clean fowl, and offered burnt offerings on the altar."

It is interesting to note that Noah, the patriarch, is leading his assembled family in a prayer of thankfulness.

His three sons, Shem, Ham, and Japheth, stand on one side of the altar and their wives on the opposite side, thus carrying out the Hebrew custom of separating the men and the women at a religious ceremony. Noah's wife occupies a place at the end of the altar, opposite Noah.

There are no children in this scene, for Biblical history states that none of Noah's three sons had any children at the time of the Flood.

The dramatic incident of the sacrifice has given the artist a rare opportunity to contrast the barrenness of the mountain peaks with the bright colors of the Hebrew garments.

Note that one of Noah's sons wears a headband instead of the customary turban, and that Noah's wife wears a veil reaching far down her back.

In the lower left-hand corner of the painting may be seen the spike driven into a crevice of the rock as a mooring for the ark. This was necessary since not all the waters had abated, and the ark might otherwise have floated away.

The Lord was pleased with Noah's sacrifice, and He blessed him and his family. He also promised never again to send a flood to destroy the earth. As a token of the covenant between Him and Noah, He "set his bow in the cloud." A faint glimpse of the rainbow may be seen reaching down to the waters.

NOAH'S SACRIFICE

Noah builded an altar unto the Lord; . . .
and offered burnt offerings on the altar.

—*Gen. 8:20.*

BRAM and his wife, Sarai, dwelt near the oaks of Mamre at Hebron, where he built an altar to God. Abram was very very rich in "cattle, in silver, and in gold."

The Lord was pleased with Abram, for he was a great and good man. Although Abram had overcome the kings of Sodom and Gomorrah and had rescued his kinsman Lot, he was depressed, for he and his wife Sarai were childless.

He was also concerned at the thought of the powerful enemies he had made through his rescue of Lot. To remove that fear, we are told in the fifteenth chapter of Genesis, the word of the Lord came to him in a vision. He heard a voice saying, "Fear not, Abram: I am thy shield, and thy exceeding great reward."

Abram was puzzled, but Josephus, the great interpreter of Jewish history, points out that Abram answered, "And what advantage will it be to me to have such rewards, when I have none to enjoy them after me?"

The Lord then assured Abram that despite his and Sarai's advanced years,

a son would be born to them and that his descendants would be very numerous.

The Bible states that God brought Abram forth from his tent and, under the canopy of night, spoke to him the prophetic words of Gen. 15:5.

Abram is shown sitting before his tent, his noble face upraised to the star-filled heavens. His eagerness to receive God's promise and his reverent attitude show plainly in his upturned face. Notice that his powerful, half-closed hand seems to be reaching out to grasp, as it were, the message. A colorful scarf is thrown carelessly over his shoulders to protect him from the cool desert air.

Sarai remains within the tent, no doubt busy with the water jars, and so does not hear the Lord's voice telling Abram to "look now toward heaven, and tell the stars, if thou be able to number them." Then the voice continues, "So shall thy seed be." And Abram believed the Lord and offered a sacrifice to Him.

Later God talked with Abram, telling him, "Thou shalt be a father of many nations."

ABRAM COUNTING THE STARS

And he brought him forth abroad, and said,
Look now toward heaven, and tell the stars, if
thou be able to number them: and he said unto
him, So shall thy seed be. And he believed in the
Lord; and he counted it to him for righteousness.

—*Gen. 15:5, 6.*

LOT AND HIS DAUGHTERS ❧ ❧

THE expression, "As wicked as Sodom and Gomorrah," has come, through the ages, to refer to any place where great wickedness and corruption exist.

These two cities of the Plain were, in Biblical times, so wicked that God several times threatened to destroy them. Abram, now known as Abraham, pleaded with the Lord to spare Sodom, and the Lord promised to do so if ten righteous people could be found among the inhabitants.

Not enough righteous people could be found in Sodom, where Lot and his wife and two daughters dwelt, or in Gomorrah; so the Lord sent two angels to descend on Gomorrah and to destroy the cities for their sins.

The angels warned Lot, who was one of the few righteous people in Sodom, to take his family and to escape before God destroyed the city. In addition to Lot's two daughters at home, he also had married daughters, but their husbands would not believe Lot's warning, and he was obliged to leave them and their husbands behind.

In the morning the two angels urged Lot to hasten, telling him to take his wife and his two daughters and to escape for his life, but cautioned him, "Look not behind thee, neither stay thou in all the plain; escape to the mountain."

The artist has portrayed with great realism the fire and brimstone devouring the cities of Sodom and Gomorrah, where "the smoke of the country went up as the smoke of a furnace."

Fleeing from the scene are the terror-stricken Lot and his two daughters, carrying their possessions in bundles.

Very significantly Lot stands behind his daughters, his arm outthrust, protecting them from the raining fire which is consuming the cities. So strong is the storm that it has bent the young saplings growing along the way and is fanning the women's hair about their heads and blowing Lot's scarf behind his back.

But why is Lot's wife not in this little group? Why is she standing apart, her face toward the holocaust? Unfortunately, Lot's wife disobeyed the angelic command and looked back toward the city, whereupon she became a pillar of salt.

It is thought that she did not really believe that God was going to destroy the city, so she looked back, and was perhaps covered with sulphur.

The New Testament, in II Pet. 2:6, refers to the destruction of Sodom and Gomorrah as "an ensample unto those that after should live ungodly."

LOT AND HIS DAUGHTERS

The angels hastened Lot, saying, Arise, take thy wife,
and thy two daughters, . . . escape to the mountain.

—Gen. 19:15, 17.

ARAH, the wife of Abraham, at first loved Ishmael, the son of her handmaid, Hagar. But when her own son, Isaac, was born, Sarah became jealous of the boy Ishmael, who had been regarded as Abraham's heir until the birth of Isaac.

Abraham was very much grieved because Sarah insisted that Hagar and her son be sent to some distant country. God, however, comforted Abraham and told him to do as Sarah wished. He promised Abraham that He would form great nations through the descendants of both Isaac and Ishmael.

Josephus, the noted chronicler of Jewish history, relates that Abraham "commanded her [Hagar] to take a bottle of water, and a loaf of bread, and so to depart, and to take Necessity for her guide."

The Bible says that Hagar departed and wandered in the wilderness of Beer-sheba. The boy Ishmael was probably fourteen or fifteen years old at the time.

In this painting Hagar's desperate situation is plainly revealed in the distraught look she gives her son as he lies exhausted and, as she thought, dying, under the meager shade of an oriental shrub, possibly a fig tree.

The bread and water which she had received from the patriarch are spent, and in that barren land there is no means of relieving the lad's thirst and no other means of protection from the burning sun than the fig tree.

Believing that her son could not live under these conditions, Hagar sat down at a distance to await his death. As she sat, weeping and sorrowful, she thought of the promise she had received. Suddenly the voice of God told her of a well nearby where she might fill her bottle. She found the well and gave her boy a drink.

God also told her to rear the lad, and under His protection Ishmael continued to grow. He later married and "came to be the father of many people." The desert became Ishmael's home, and his descendants still claim it as their birthright.

While we may pity Hagar and her son, we realize that this story is evidence of the jealousies and unhappiness caused by polygamy, which was an accepted custom of the times.

HAGAR AND ISHMAEL

The water was spent in the bottle, and
she cast the child under one of the shrubs.

—*Gen. 21:15.*

JACOB MEETS RACHEL ઓ ઓ ઓ ઓ

ISAAC, the father of Jacob, made Jacob promise that he would not take anyone for a wife who did not serve God and that he would, therefore, try to marry a daughter of Laban, a kinsman.

On his way to Haran, where Laban lived, Jacob saw a well—perhaps the same one where Abraham's servant had seen Rebekah, Jacob's mother. A group of shepherds were there with their flocks, and when Jacob asked if they knew his uncle, he was told that Laban's daughter was coming with her father's sheep to water them. While awaiting the approach of Rachel and her flock, Jacob removed the flat stone that covered the mouth of the well, in order to be prepared to water her sheep.

What a beautiful painting the artist has created of the first meeting of the wanderer Jacob, and the lovely young girl.

As Rachel approaches Jacob, it is evident by his rapt expression that he has already fallen in love with the beautiful maiden who stands shyly before him. This tender meeting is witnessed by the two shepherds who have withdrawn to the background.

Joy, happiness, and beauty, in figures and landscape, are vividly expressed in this pastoral scene.

The romance of Jacob and his beautiful, bright-eyed and charming cousin, Rachel, is one of the most touching stories in the Old Testament.

Jacob loved Rachel with such a deep and tender love that he was willing to work for her father for seven years in order to win her as his wife.

A great wedding feast was prepared, and Jacob was overjoyed. His happiness was short-lived, for Laban cheated Jacob and would not let him take Rachel as his bride. Instead, Laban forced Rachel's older sister, Leah, upon Jacob.

Poor Jacob was in despair, as well as being bitterly angry at the deception. His uncle explained, however, that the younger daughter must never be married before the first-born. But if Jacob would toil for another seven years for nothing, Laban would then willingly give Rachel to him as his second wife.

Jacob's love for Rachel was so great that he agreed to Laban's order, and, at the end of the second seven years, Rachel became his wife.

The Bible tells us that Rachel was Jacob's favorite wife; that she bore him two sons, Joseph and Benjamin.

Rachel's death at Benjamin's birth left Jacob heartbroken, but he found great comfort in Rachel's two sons, Joseph and little Benjamin.

JACOB MEETS RACHEL

Rachel came with her father's sheep: . . . Jacob went near, and rolled
the stone from the well's mouth, and watered the flock of Laban.

—Gen. 29:9, 10.

JOSEPH SOLD BY HIS BRETHREN

THE affection and favoritism shown by Jacob to his seventeen-year-old son Joseph, born to him by Rachel, excited the envy and hatred of his brothers; so did Joseph's dreams, which he related to his father and brethren. To the envious brothers all the dreams foretold happiness and prosperity for Joseph, and superiority over them.

Jacob loved Joseph so much because of his goodness and faithfulness that he gave him a coat of bright colors. This special mark of favor made Joseph's brothers very jealous. When Joseph's two dreams were interpreted to mean that the brothers should obey him, they were enraged.

One day Jacob sent Joseph to Shechem to inquire about the welfare of his brothers, who were feeding their flocks in the fields nearby. When he reached Shechem, he discovered that his brothers had moved their flocks to Dothan, fifteen miles away. Joseph trudged on, and as he approached Dothan, he was readily seen by his brothers because of his bright coat.

At that moment a wild scheme entered the brothers' heads, and they plotted to kill Joseph and then report to their father that a wild beast had killed him. Reuben, the eldest, who felt more kindly toward Joseph but still did not dare oppose his brothers,

said, "Let us not kill him; let us cast him into this pit and leave him there."

So the brothers stripped the boy of his coat, and Reuben, we are told, let his young brother down gently into the empty pit, before leaving to seek better pasture for his flocks.

In his absence, a caravan of Midianites traveling down to Egypt drew near. Judah, another of Joseph's jealous brothers, at this moment saw an opportunity to sell Joseph.

Joseph was drawn from the pit and sold to the merchantmen for twenty pieces of silver. In this painting young Joseph, stripped to the waist, hands bound with rope, is standing forlorn and frightened as one of the merchants passes the sale money to one of Joseph's brothers.

Judah, the perpetrator of the plot, sits carelessly on the edge of the pit, in the act of bargaining with the merchants for a higher price for the boy.

One merchant, seated on the ground, appears to be appraising the boy, wondering no doubt whether he is strong enough to become a slave and worth the price paid. The opulent merchant who keeps a firm grasp on the moneybag shrewdly and somewhat reluctantly holds the money over the upturned palm of the eager brother.

Every phase of this incident portrays only too well the sins of avarice and family jealousy.

JOSEPH SOLD BY HIS BRETHREN

They stript Joseph out of his coat, his coat of many
colors that was on him; . . . and cast him into a pit.

—Gen. 37:23, 24.

JOSEPH INTERPRETS PHARAOH'S DREAM

POTIPHAR, chief officer to Pharaoh, the king of Egypt, bought Joseph from the Midianite merchants and installed him in his house as overseer. For some years Joseph continued to live in Potiphar's home, a slave in name, but really the master of Potiphar's affairs.

Then Joseph was imprisoned after being falsely accused by Potiphar's wife because he would not do wrong.

In the prison with Joseph were two other slaves: Pharaoh's chief butler and his chief baker. Each of these two men had a strange dream which Joseph interpreted. The butler's dream seemed to indicate that he would be restored to favor; the baker's, that he would be hanged upon a tree. Knowing that he could expect little help from the latter, Joseph urged the butler to speak to the king for him, for he, Joseph, had done no wrong.

Joseph's interpretations came true, and the butler was restored to his old place. One would suppose that the butler would have remembered Joseph, who had given him a promise of freedom, but in his gladness he forgot all about Joseph.

Two years later, while Joseph was still in prison, Pharaoh himself had two strange dreams. He sent for his wise men, but not one of them was able to explain the meaning of the dreams. Suddenly the butler remembered Joseph, and he suggested that Joseph be brought to interpret the king's dreams. Joseph was now about thirty years of age.

Joseph was taken out of prison, after which he shaved off his beard so as to be ceremonially clean in the king's presence. He was dressed in new garments and led into Pharaoh's presence.

Here in this scene are shown the trappings of an Egyptian potentate. The Pharaoh in his richly embroidered robes and jeweled armlets and belt sits on his throne over which a coverlet of leopard skin is thrown. Behind him a slave girl gently swings an ostrich fan back and forth to cool the air, while another slave strums a kind of harp, the typical instrument of music of early Biblical times. One of the king's counselors, standing in the shadows, is watching Joseph appraisingly. Perhaps he is hoping that Joseph can interpret the dream.

When Joseph explained that the king's dream foretold of a famine, the king wondered at the discretion and wisdom of Joseph, and later set him to rule over the land of Egypt because he was able to advise the king how to prepare for the famine which would follow the seven years of plenty.

JOSEPH INTERPRETS PHARAOH'S DREAM

Then Pharaoh sent and called Joseph, and they brought him
hastily out of the dungeon: and he . . . came in unto Pharaoh.

—Gen. 41:14.

SOME time after Joseph had been made ruler over the land of Egypt, he brought his father Jacob, and all his family, including Joseph's eleven brothers and all their families, down to Egypt from Canaan because of a famine in their own country.

Joseph then took his father, who was by this time a very old man, to see Pharaoh, and Jacob gave his blessing to the king.

Jacob lived to be almost one hundred and fifty years old, and when he was about to die, Joseph went to comfort him and to receive his blessing.

Joseph took his two sons Ephraim and Manasseh with him so that they too could receive their grandfather's blessing.

It was the custom in those days to place the right hand on the head of the first-born and the left hand on the head of the younger.

Jacob's eyes were dim with age, and he could not see the two boys clearly as they stood before him. As shown here in the painting, the venerable Jacob is blessing Ephraim and Manasseh but crossing his hands as he does so, thus placing his right hand on Ephraim, the younger, and his left on Manasseh, the older.

Joseph, who wants the greater blessing to go to Manasseh, is displeased and reaches out his hand in an attempt to move his father's hand from Ephraim's head to Manasseh's.

Jacob, wise old patriarch that he was, refuses to allow Joseph to disturb the arrangement, saying, "I know it, my son, I know it. God will bless the older son but the greater blessing shall be with the younger, for from him shall come a multitude of nations."

One can see, however, that Joseph, even though he respects Jacob, has a scheming look on his face as he glances apprehensively at the old patriarch whose eyes are dimmed with age.

The Bible tells us that after Jacob blessed Ephraim and Manasseh, he called all his sons together and told them, being instructed by God, what should happen to them in their latter days. Then he was "gathered unto his people."

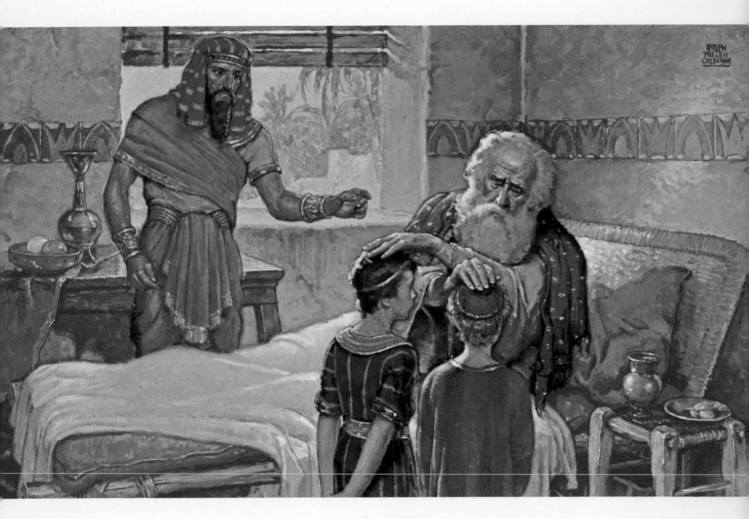

JACOB BLESSES JOSEPH'S SONS

Israel stretched out his right hand, and laid it upon Ephraim's head, who was the younger, and his left hand upon Manasseh's head, guiding his hands wittingly; for Manasseh was the firstborn.

—Gen. 48:14.

THE ADOPTION OF MOSES ❧ ❧ ❧

THE story of the rescue of the baby Moses reads like a romance of divine providence. The ruling Pharaoh, jealous of the success of the Israelites, had ordered that all Hebrew male children be put to death at birth. When his order was defied, he issued an edict that every son born to Hebrew parents should be cast into the Nile.

Jochebed, mother of the baby Moses, defied the cruel order of the Pharaoh and hid her baby boy for three months, until it was no longer possible to conceal him. She then wove a little cradle, or ark, as it was called, of the bulrushes that grew along the banks of the Nile and covered it with pitch to make it watertight. She placed her baby son in it after wrapping him in soft cloths, and carefully set the little cradle afloat near the low bank of the river.

With the faith of a good mother that the child would be discovered, she returned home and then sent Miriam, the baby's sister, to see what might happen.

Then it was that the Princess Thermuthis, with her attendants, came to bathe in the cooling waters of the sacred Nile. The floating cradle drifted close by the royal group. The princess had the cradle brought to her and opened. At that moment the child cried, and the heart of the daughter of Pharaoh was touched, and she took the babe in her arms. Miriam stood nearby and shrewdly offered to find a Hebrew woman to nurse the baby. Princess Thermuthis agreed to the proposal, and the child was entrusted to his joyful mother.

In this painting we have a vivid picture of the ritual of bathing as observed by royalty. So that Pharaoh's daughter might have the privacy accorded her rank, a tent was set up in which she could disrobe. A Nubian slave, in the Egyptian garb of that period, stood with poised flabellum, or fan, to create a breeze, for the Egyptian sun and sands were burning hot. The decorated chest was used to carry towels and robes, as well as the jars of salves which appear in the foreground.

Note the eagerness in Miriam's face as she approaches the princess, and the compassionate smile of Pharaoh's daughter as she nestles the baby in her arms.

In the progress of time the child was taken back to the palace and adopted by the princess. And she called him Moses, because he had been drawn out of the water.

THE ADOPTION OF MOSES

The daughter of Pharaoh came down to wash herself at the river;
. . . and when she saw the ark among the flags, she sent her maid
to fetch it. And when she had opened it, she saw the child.

—*Ex. 2:5, 6.*

OD had spoken from the mountain as "with a voice of thunder" the words of the Ten Commandments. When the people heard the voice of the Lord and saw Mount Sinai smoking and flashing lightning, they were frightened. They appealed to Moses, their leader, not to let God speak to them, for His voice frightened them, but for Him to speak to Moses, and then Moses would speak God's words to the people.

God then called Moses to the top of Mount Sinai, where he stayed alone with God for forty days. And God gave to Moses two tablets of stone upon which He had written with His own hand the Ten Commandments.

Day after day passed, and Moses still stayed on the mountain. The people became alarmed and went to Aaron, Moses' brother, and said to him, "We do not know what has become of Moses, so why do you not make us a god to worship and lead us, as Moses did, out of Egypt?"

Aaron, unlike Moses, was not a man of strong will, so he took the people's gold and earrings, melted them down and made a molten calf of them and built an altar before the image.

The people danced and feasted around it, until the Lord spoke to Moses in the mountain, ordering him to hasten down from the mount as He was about to destroy His people for their faithlessness.

Moses pleaded with God, and God did not destroy the people. Instead, He sent Moses down to them with the two tables in his hand.

Here we see Moses as he draws near to the altar and discovers the appalling situation. The people have been dancing and feasting, but they stop their singing and idolatry and gather around Moses. The faces of those standing near the golden calf express fear and wonderment and even shame.

Moses, the mighty lawgiver, is so angry because of the wickedness of his people that he raises the tablets of stone high above his head and casts them down with such force that they break into pieces on the rocks.

Aaron, Moses' brother, who was responsible for letting the people persuade him to make the golden calf, cowers behind Moses, his hand halfway to his face, possibly to shield himself from the flying pieces of stone. The righteous anger of a mighty man of God is purposely contrasted with the soulless graven image on the altar.

The glow in the sky behind the purple tints of Mount Sinai shows that God's presence is still in the mountain.

MOSES BREAKS THE TABLES

Moses' anger waxed hot, and he cast the tables out of his hands, and brake them beneath the mount.

—*Ex. 32:19*.

THE REPORT OF THE SPIES 〜 〜 〜

THE Israelites camped near Mount Sinai for nearly a year after God gave Moses the laws by which the people were to live. The pillar of cloud by day and the pillar of fire by night stayed over them as they worked, building the Tabernacle and learning the laws.

At last the cloud rose up, and the people knew this was the sign for them to move on. Led by the cloud and the pillar of fire, they moved toward the promised Land of Canaan. They stopped at a place called Kadesh, where they found springs of water and grass for their cattle.

As they camped, God told Moses to send some men into Canaan to see what kind of land it was, what kind of fruit and crops grew in it, what the people were like, and whether they were strong or weak. Accordingly, Moses sent out twelve men, one from each of the twelve tribes of Israel, to spy out the land. One of these men was Joshua, and another was Caleb.

Near the brook of Eshcol they found a cluster of grapes so large that two of the spies had to carry it on a staff between their shoulders. The spies also brought back pomegranates, a fruit about the size of an orange with a bright red pulp, and full of juice.

The spies also reported that the cities of Canaan were walled and that the people were very strong. When the Israelites heard this they were frightened, and they began to lift up their voices against Moses and his brother Aaron, crying out that it would have been better had they stayed in Egypt.

Joshua and Caleb remonstrated with the people, begging them not to rebel against the Lord or to fear the Canaanites. Instead of listening to the advice of Caleb and Joshua, the people prepared to stone them.

At that moment the glory of the Lord appeared before the people, and God spoke to Moses, telling him that He would punish the people and disinherit them so that they would never possess the Promised Land.

In the painting we see Moses pleading with God for his people. He is asking the Lord to pardon the Israelites as He had done before when they had offended Him. You may be sure that God heard Moses' prayer, as He hears the prayers of all His followers, but He told Moses that only Joshua and Caleb would be permitted to enter the Promised Land. The people were to turn back to the desert, where they were to wander for nearly forty years.

This painting is one of sharp contrasts. Here we see Moses and Aaron, both strong of body and reverent in attitude, and behind them, some of the Israelites who cringe and peer with distrustful eyes upon their leader.

THE REPORT OF THE SPIES

They . . . cut down from thence a branch with one cluster
of grapes, and they bare it between two upon a staff.

—Num. 13:23.

JOSHUA COMMANDS THE SUN

So the sun stood still in the midst of heaven,
and hasted not to go down about a whole day.

—*Josh. 10:13.*

JOSHUA COMMANDS THE SUN ❧ ❧

AFTER the death of Moses, Joshua led the Children of Israel into the Promised Land; later, in a succession of campaigns, he captured Jericho and Ai. Fearful of being destroyed by the Israelites, the Gibeonites, who were the inhabitants of four small cities in that region and named from their chief city, Gibeon, deceitfully became allied with the Israelites. But in three days the deception became known to the Israelites, and they punished them by making slaves of them.

After the people of Gibeon had submitted to Israel, the king of Jerusalem banded together with four other kings to march against Gibeon. Joshua had given his word that he would not kill the Gibeonites and would not, if he could help it, let others kill them. So he marched all night to Gibeon with his army, assured of God's help.

After a march up rugged hills, Joshua began the battle against the five kings very early in the morning. Before noon, the enemy was in full retreat down the steep slopes of Beth-horon. As they fled before the Israelites, the Lord caused great hailstones to rain down on them, and these stones "killed many more than the Israelites had slain."

Joshua, standing on the summit west of Gibeon not yet reached by the storm and fearing that the enemy might escape, is shown as he utters his dramatic command.

God hearkened unto the voice of a man: The sun stood still, the hailstorm ceased, and daylight lasted until the Israelites vanquished the foe.

The artist has created a figure of might and power in the towering stance of Joshua, who dominates the center of the painting. But despite the leader's physical strength, it is only with divine help that he is able to command the sun to do his will.

GIDEON'S SACRIFICE ❧ ❧ ❧ ❧ ❧

DESPITE God's warnings, the "children of Israel again did evil in the sight of the Lord." Even Joash, the father of Gideon, erected an altar to the false god Baal in a grove of trees where the Midianites would not discover it.

The Israelites, in their despair at the cruel treatment of the Midianites, again cried to God, so the Lord sent an angel to Gideon, commanding him to throw down his father's altar and to cut down the grove that was planted around it, and to build an altar to Him and sacrifice his father's bullock, or young ox, on it.

Afraid to do so by day, Gideon went out by night and took ten of his father's servants. First he threw down the image of Baal and cut in pieces the wooden image of Asherah, a Canaanite goddess, and destroyed the altar before those idols. In its place he built an altar to God and on it laid the remains of the idols, and also a bullock, as a sacrifice.

In this painting the flame from the burning idols and the burnt offering lights up the night sky and reflects in the faces of the surrounding group of men.

The figure of Gideon stands out; the fleece, symbol of his judgeship, is about his shoulders, his arms are upraised as a promise to his people and to his God.

GIDEON'S SACRIFICE

Then Gideon took ten men of his servants,
and did as the Lord had said unto him.

—Judg. 6:27.

SAMSON AND DELILAH ❧ ❧ ❧ ❧

URING the war between the Israelites and the Philistines, Samson rose up to deliver the Israelites from their enemy. Great and powerful as Samson was, however, he let his love for a sinful woman named Delilah bring about his downfall.

The chiefs of the Philistines promised a great reward to Delilah if she could discover the source of Samson's strength. She willingly agreed to the proposal, and three times she pleaded with Samson to tell her his secret. But Samson was unwilling to reveal this, and three times he baffled her and was able to free himself.

Delilah persisted day after day by referring to his love for her, until finally Samson, in a moment of weakness, disclosed the source of his great strength. He told her that he was a Nazirite; that if he were shaven, his God-given strength would leave him.

The false Delilah called the lords of the Philistines again and asked them to come once more, as Samson had at last bared his heart and had told her the source of his unusual strength.

When Samson fell asleep, Delilah called for a man to shave off Samson's locks.

The artist has pictured this scene of transgression and treachery with great faithfulness to the incident. Samson, the once unconquerable giant, is about to be deprived of his source of strength. As he lies on a richly upholstered couch in an obvious stupor, amid luxurious surroundings and appointments, the treacherous Delilah beckons to the approaching Philistine.

Cruelty shows on the face of the man about to shave off Samson's locks and in the leer of the Philistine half hiding behind the silken draperies.

Delilah's pronouncement, "The Philistines be upon thee, Samson," awoke Samson, but by that time his seven locks had been shaved off, and his strength had departed from him and he could not defend himself against his enemies.

The Bible relates that the "Philistines took him, and put out his eyes, and brought him down to Gaza," where he ground corn in the prison.

Samson deserves to be admired for his courage and strength; on the other hand, he is to be pitied because of his weakness to resist temptation.

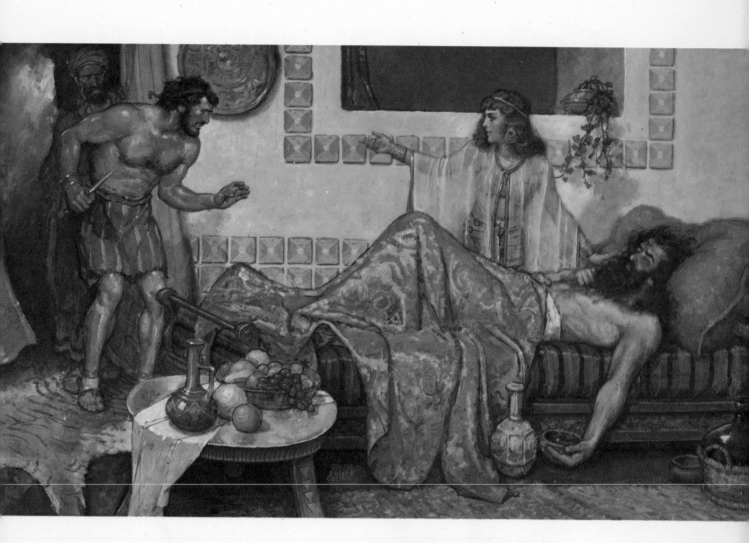

SAMSON AND DELILAH

She called for a man, and she caused him
to shave off the seven locks of his head.

—Judg. 16:19.

RUTH CLAVE UNTO NAOMI ❧ ❧ ❧

THE devotion of a young woman for her mother-in-law provides one of the most interesting historical romances of the Bible.

During a time of famine in Israel, a Jewish farmer named Elimelech took his wife Naomi and his two sons to dwell in the fertile land of Moab across the Dead Sea. The sons married two Moabite women, Ruth and Orpah. About ten years later both Elimelech and the sons died, and Naomi was left in a strange country with her widowed daughters-in-law. Naomi longed for her old home, for the Moabites among whom she lived did not serve God, and she, who was an Israelite, could not feel happy there.

Having learned that there was now food enough in her homeland, she set out to see it once more, and her two daughters-in-law accompanied her on the journey.

In this painting, with the rich land of Moab as a background, we see an interesting grouping of women: Naomi, advanced in years; with her Ruth, in the bloom of youth. The third, whose back is turned, and who tradition tells us is Orpah, is also a young woman, widowed as was Ruth.

Naomi has from time to time en-treated her two beloved daughters-in-law to return to their mothers' homes in Moab. Sobbing, they both refuse to do so. Naomi persists in her request, and after a tender farewell, Orpah at last leaves Naomi and Ruth to go back to her homeland.

Ruth remains with her mother-in-law and, after casting aside her bundle of belongings and falling to her knees, her hands clasping those of Naomi, she utters those memorable words, "In-treat me not to leave thee, or to return from following after thee: for whither thou goest, I will go; and where thou lodgest, I will lodge: thy people shall be my people, and thy God my God."

Beauty of character as well as of face are given young Ruth in this painting. At the same time a slight smile of happiness lights up Naomi's countenance, for Ruth's devotion and decision have brought great pleasure to her.

The Bible tells us that Ruth was later befriended by a wealthy man named Boaz, whom she married. Through Ruth and Boaz descended the royal line of David, and on down to our Saviour, Jesus Christ, who was called the Son of David.

Christians see in Ruth the working out of a divine purpose.

RUTH CLAVE UNTO NAOMI

Ruth said, Intreat me not to leave thee, or to return from following after thee: for whither thou goest, I will go.

—*Ruth 1:16*.

HANNAH PRESENTING SAMUEL TO ELI

THE artist's love for little children is very apparent in this touching and dramatic scene of Hannah presenting her little son to Eli, the high priest, in fulfilment of her vow.

Among the goodly company who went to the Tabernacle in Shiloh to worship were Elkanah and his wife Hannah. Hannah was childless, and her heart was grieved.

In her sorrow she poured out her soul to God and made a vow that if God gave her a male child, she would give him to the Lord all the days of his life.

Hannah's vow was fulfilled and she kept her promise, for as soon as the little boy, whose name was Samuel, which meant "asked of God," was old enough to be separated from his mother, he was taken to the Tabernacle.

The strength of Hannah's faith is plainly visible in her noble bearing and her reverent attitude as she kneels behind her child and expresses her faith in her song of dedication, "As long as he liveth he shall be lent to the Lord."

Although little Samuel was wholly unaware of the responsibilities he was to assume, we see him as he trustingly stands before the high priest, his little hands clasped in front of his linen ephod.

Eli's attire is rich in material and color and design as befitting his official position as high priest. His headdress, made in turban form and banded with a fillet, bears the customary inscription, "Holiness to the Lord."

The rich furnishings of the interior of the Tabernacle at Shiloh are shown in glowing color in this painting. The six-pointed star, a symbol of Jewish belief, is repeated in the various appointments.

The roll or scroll, made of parchment or skin, which rests on the low table beside the seat of the high priest, possibly contained the history of the nation. The fact that the scroll is partially unrolled indicates that Eli had been reading it when Hannah brought little Samuel into the high priest's presence.

Hannah was abundantly rewarded for her faith, for every year as she and her husband went to the Tabernacle to offer their sacrifices, she could see her son grow in wisdom and in favor with God and man.

HANNAH PRESENTING SAMUEL TO ELI

For this child I prayed; . . . as long as
he liveth he shall be lent to the Lord.

—*I Sam. 1: 27, 28.*

AMUEL, the great Hebrew prophet and judge, mourned for King Saul, whom the Lord had rejected as king of Israel. But the Lord told Samuel to stop grieving for Saul and to journey to Bethlehem to the home of Jesse, son of Obed. There Samuel was to anoint one of Jesse's sons as the future king.

Samuel was afraid that Saul, aware that God was displeased with his conduct, would try to kill him. The Lord told Samuel to take with him a heifer as a sacrifice and if anyone should ask him why he was going to Bethlehem he should reply that he was going to make a sacrifice before the Lord.

When Samuel had prepared the sacrifice, he called Jesse and his sons to partake of it. Then Jesse caused seven of his sons to pass before Samuel. The eldest son was a tall, handsome man, and Samuel thought that he must certainly be the one God had chosen to be king. However, God told Samuel that He did not look on outward appearances, but at the heart; and that Eliab was not the chosen man.

One after another, seven of Jesse's sons passed before Samuel. All these men were stalwart and fine-looking, but Samuel said to Jesse, "The Lord hath not chosen these." Then Samuel asked Jesse whether he had any other sons besides the seven. Jesse said he had one more, David, the youngest— a shepherd who took care of the flocks. Samuel then told Jesse to call David immediately, for no one could sit down to the feast until he came.

When comely David appeared, Samuel knew, within his heart, that this was the one God had chosen to be king. The Lord spoke and said, "Arise, anoint him: for this is he."

The painting shows the white-haired prophet pouring oil from the little horn-shaped vessel over the head of the kneeling shepherd boy. David's ruddy complexion, his shepherd's garb and his shepherd's crook show that he no doubt had hurried in from the fields to the prophet's presence.

The venerable Jesse, hands resting on his staff, seems to be pondering over God's choice, as he watches intently. In the faces of the seven rejected brothers we can see a variety of emotions: anger, hatred, scorn, surprise.

Obviously, David's brothers are not pleased with the choice of the new king. David, however, accepts the honor with calm dignity. And from that day forward the Spirit of the Lord came upon David.

Aside from its richness of design and color, this painting is a remarkable character study—a source of endless speculation and human interest.

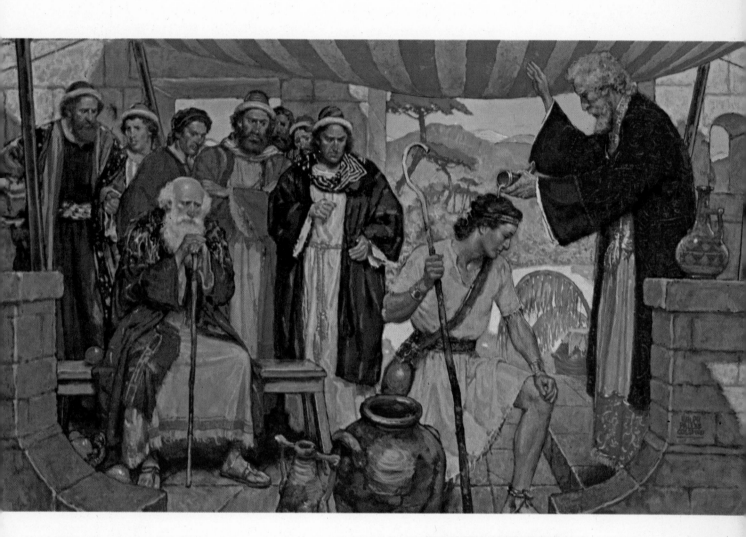

DAVID ANOINTED

Then Samuel took the horn of oil, and anointed him in the midst of his brethren: and the Spirit of the Lord came upon David from that day forward.

—*I Sam. 16:13.*

FRIENDSHIP OF DAVID AND JONATHAN

ONE of the greatest friendships ever recorded, either in Biblical history or in all literature, is that between Jonathan, eldest son of King Saul, and David, son of Jesse.

This friendship began on the day of David's return from his victory over Goliath and continued till Jonathan's death.

David had been brought to King Saul's house, and there he met Jonathan, Saul's son, for the first time. It was then "that the soul of Jonathan was knit with the soul of David, and Jonathan loved him as his own soul."

The devotion of these two friends has given rise to the term "a David and Jonathan friendship."

Here we see Jonathan and David meeting in the wood near the hill-town of Ziph, where they made a covenant before the Lord.

Jonathan is dressed in regal scarlet and purple robes befitting the son of a king, whereas David wears the simple garb of the shepherd. Notice the water flask slung across his shoulder by a leather thong, and the shepherd's staff.

As a token of his love for David, and as a bond of their friendship, Jonathan has removed his girdle and, winding it around his sword, is presenting both to his friend.

Alongside the tree rests Jonathan's bow and his shield. The shield, sometimes known as a buckler, was carried by archers, and varied in shape. Jonathan's shield was round, and possibly made of leather, covered with brass bands. Perhaps Jonathan also gave his bow to his friend, although there is no mention of this in the Bible.

David, shepherd's crook in his left hand, responds gladly to Jonathan's overtures, as the former's outstretched hand seems to indicate.

We are told that David possessed great physical strength, which, in this painting, is strongly emphasized, as is also his ruddy complexion.

A sheep, which is a symbol of affection in the Bible, looks placidly toward her master, while the lamb nestles close to its mother for protection.

The Bible tells us that Jonathan's act of friendship "strengthened his hand in God."

When King Saul and Jonathan and two other of Saul's sons were later slain in battle by the Philistines, David grieved over the death of his most faithful friend and his father.

The honor he paid to Saul and to Jonathan is given in the Second Book of Samuel, chapter 1:19-27. It is one of the most beautiful lamentations in history, in which David refers to Jonathan as his "brother."

FRIENDSHIP OF DAVID AND JONATHAN

Then Jonathan and David made a covenant, because he loved him as his own soul.

—*I Sam. 18:3.*

GOLIATH'S CHALLENGE

It came to pass, when the Philistine arose, and came and drew nigh to meet David, that David hasted, and ran toward the army to meet the Philistine. And David put his hand in his bag, and took thence a stone, and slang it, and smote the Philistine in his forehead, that the stone sunk into his forehead; and he fell upon his face to the earth.

—*I Sam. 17:48, 49.*

GOLIATH'S CHALLENGE ❧ ❧ ❧ ❧

AGAIN the Israelites and the Philistines were at war, and the Philistines were full of courage, for in their camp was a terrible giant named Goliath.

This daring and formidable man, about ten feet tall, challenged the Israelites to send a man to fight him. Should the Israelites win, the Philistines would be their servants; but if not, the Israelites would serve the Philistines.

David, the brave young shepherd lad, offered to slay the giant, so Saul the king put his own armor on David. David, however, insisted it must be taken off. "Let me fight the giant in my own way," he declared. Young, slim as a reed, but bold in heart, he had no weapon save his sturdy shepherd's staff and a sling.

With his hair blowing in the wind, feet apart to steady himself, David is prepared with the Lord's help to direct the stone to a vulnerable spot on Goliath's broad forehead.

Opposite him the Philistine giant stands in his protective armor. He is dressed in a coat of mail, a sort of jacket or shirt of brass. On his legs are greaves, or thin plates of metal, to protect the front of the legs below the knee.

In his hand he carries a spear, more than twice the size of David's staff. On his head is a heavy brass helmet, and in his left hand he carries an enormous shield.

Defiant, mocking, and with assurance that in a few moments he could laugh at the folly of the Israelites in sending a boy to fight him, Goliath moves to meet his adversary.

NAAMAN'S WIFE AND HER HANDMAID

NAAMAN, captain of the host of Ben-hadad, king of Syria, was afflicted with leprosy. Naaman's wife had a young female servant who had been brought captive out of the land of Israel on one of the Syrian raids into that country.

When the little maid saw her master's suffering she said to her mistress, "Would God my lord were with the prophet that is in Samaria! for he would recover him of his leprosy."

The speech of the little captive maid was reported to Naaman, who in turn told his royal master, who wrote a letter of introduction and sent him to the king of Israel.

The king of Israel burst into a rage when he read the letter, exclaiming, "Am I God, to kill and to make alive?" He feared that Ben-hadad would quarrel with him if he failed to cure Naaman. When Elisha heard what had happened, he begged the king to send Naaman to him.

When Naaman arrived at Elisha's door, a messenger told the captain to wash in the Jordan seven times and he would be made clean. At first Naaman was angry, but when his servants suggested he try Elisha's remedy, he did and was made clean.

The faith of a young girl and the ever-present power of God, administered through His prophet, turned the idolater Naaman into a worshiper of Jehovah.

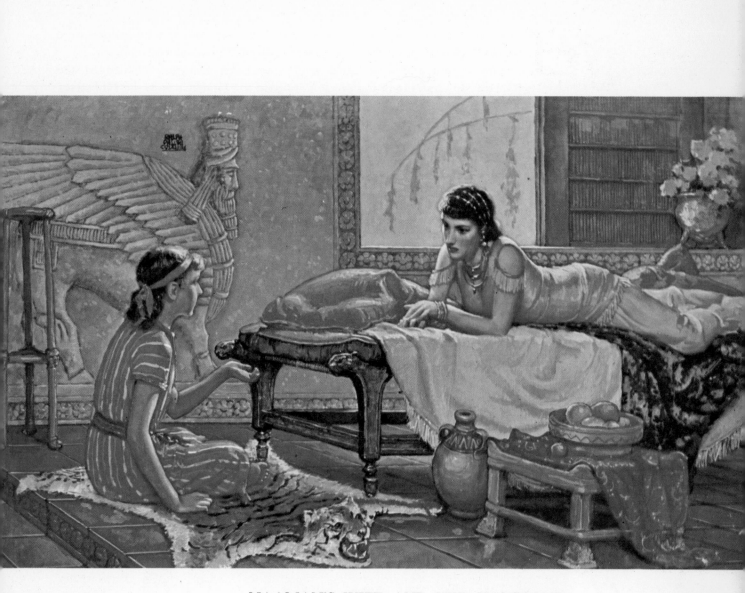

NAAMAN'S WIFE AND HER HANDMAID

Would God my lord were with the prophet that is
in Samaria! for he would recover him of his leprosy.

—*II Kings 5:3.*

ESTHER BEFORE KING AHASUERUS

FTER the Jews were permitted to return to their own land, many of them still remained in Persia. Among these was Mordecai, who lived in the royal city of Shushan with Esther, his cousin, who "was fair and beautiful."

A great feast was being held in Shushan, and the king, Ahasuerus, ordered his wife, Queen Vashti, to appear before the revelers. The queen refused and was banished from the throne. The king then decreed that all the young maidens in the realm should be brought together so that one could be chosen to replace Vashti.

Esther was selected and took her place as queen, without anyone's knowing that she was a Jewess. She had come to the Persian throne at a critical time, for a conspiracy against the king was discovered by Mordecai.

Esther told King Ahasuerus of the plot to assassinate him, and the instigators were discovered and hanged. Naturally this discovery increased Esther's influence over the king.

About this time a royal favorite, Haman, was given a position of great importance, that of "prime minister" over the empire. Everyone in a subordinate position was ordered by the king to bow down to Haman. This Mordecai refused to do, so Haman obtained from the king a decree to massacre everyone of the Jewish faith.

Mordecai urged the queen to intercede for her people. But she was afraid, for she knew that no one could enter the king's presence without his command, on penalty of death. If, however, the king held out his golden scepter, the penalty was not exacted.

Here we see Esther, clothed in her royal apparel and wearing a queenly crown, as she approaches the throne. Her eagerness to touch the golden scepter held out to her shows in the outstretched arm and open hand. The king seems ready to welcome her, yet there is a look of questioning in his deep-set dark eyes! He may have been overpowered by her beauty, for he promised her anything she asked.

The Bible tells us that following Esther's dramatic triumph, the king promised to confer on Mordecai some signal mark of his favor. Meanwhile, Haman had contrived to have Mordecai hanged.

When Ahasuerus found out about Haman's diabolical plot, he commanded him to be hanged instead of Mordecai. So it was Haman who was eventually humiliated and Mordecai honored, and in addition the Jewish race was spared.

ESTHER BEFORE KING AHASUERUS

The king held out to Esther the golden sceptre that was in his
hand. So Esther drew near, and touched the top of the sceptre.

—*Esth. 5:2.*

DARIUS the Mede was about sixty-two years old when he was made king of the Chaldeans. He set one hundred and twenty satraps or princes over the kingdom who were subject to three presidents, of whom Daniel was one.

Jealousy arose among all the others, and they sought to discredit Daniel, because Darius entrusted him with everything. But Daniel was above temptation, and those who envied him could find no fault in him.

However, when they saw that Daniel prayed to God three times a day, they conspired among themselves to ruin him. They petitioned the king to issue a proclamation that any person offering a prayer to any god or any man, except to the king, for thirty days, should be cast into the den of lions.

Darius, never suspecting that this was a plot against Daniel, signed the decree. Of course everyone except Daniel respected the law. Daniel, as was his wont, stood and prayed to God three times a day before the open window of his house. The princes reported Daniel's actions to Darius and, distressed though he was, the king was compelled to cast Daniel into the den of lions, because Daniel's enemies insisted that the law of the Medes and Persians was inviolate.

The Jewish historian Josephus relates that Darius hoped God would deliver Daniel, and that "he would undergo nothing that was terrible by the wild beasts."

When Daniel was cast into the den, Darius put his seal to the stone at the opening and went his way. The king spent a miserable night and in the early morning he hastened to the den. He called to Daniel and was overjoyed to hear him say, "My God hath sent his angel, and hath shut the lions' mouths."

In the painting of this scene the artist has placed the figure of Daniel in the forefront, where the light from the barred opening shows the calm, untroubled face of the prophet, his faith unwavering. Even the lions and lionesses seem unconcerned at the presence of the man, and the cub is trusting enough to lie at Daniel's feet.

Only a water jar and a bowl bear evidence of any sustenance having been given to Daniel. The blanched bone in the foreground is mute evidence that the lions had previously eaten of animal or human flesh, but had spared Daniel.

Because Daniel had believed in his God, he had not been harmed.

DANIEL IN THE DEN OF LIONS

My God hath sent his angel, and hath shut the
lions' mouths, that they have not hurt me.

—*Dan. 6:22.*

The New Testament

JOSEPH AND MARY AT THE INN

OSEPH and Mary had traveled over fifty long, weary miles from Nazareth to Bethlehem to be counted for the census, Mary riding on a donkey, Joseph walking alongside.

As the day drew to a close, the pair approached the city of Bethlehem. Joseph, fully aware that Mary was fatigued and unable to travel much farther, sought lodging at an inn. But the inn was already fully occupied when they arrived.

The landlord, noting Mary's condition of approaching motherhood, realized that some place must be provided for her to rest.

The only place he had to offer Mary and Joseph was a rude shelter, or stable, which may have been, as tradition states, in a cave or grotto.

Leading the couple down the steps into the shelter, the landlord, lantern in hand, points out a spot where Joseph and Mary may rest.

It is evident that Joseph is not pleased about the accommodations, for we see him protesting by upraised left hand, disappointment showing plainly on his troubled face. In his right hand he carries their meager possessions tied in a crude bundle.

Mary, on the other hand, appears serene and calm, and her lovely countenance bespeaks the inner grace with which she has accepted the honor of being chosen to be the mother of the Messiah.

The colorful robes of Joseph and of the elderly white-haired landlord dramatically highlight the interior of the dingy stable, soon to be the scene of the Nativity.

At the entrance we see the figure of another traveler. Perhaps he, too, has been turned away from the inn and is waiting to see whether the landlord will permit him also to sleep in the stable. It may be supposed, however, that only Joseph and Mary occupied the shelter that night, which was indeed a lowly place for the birthplace of the Messiah.

This particular scene has rarely been depicted, but in this portrayal it becomes a moment of great significance. This is illustration at its artistic best, since it provides an intimate glimpse of things which are only suggested in the written account.

JOSEPH AND MARY AT THE INN

There was no room for them in the inn.

—Luke 2:7.

THE SHEPHERDS ON THE HILLSIDE

Throughout the ages, in sacred song and in art, the beautiful Christmas story of the shepherds watching over their flocks by night has oft been repeated. And yet the Gospel of Luke is the only Gospel that tells the story of the shepherds.

In keeping with the humble origin of Jesus, it was fitting that the divine announcement of His birth should have been made to a group of shepherds on a Judean hillside.

Tradition states that the shepherds who tended the flocks at Bethlehem occupied a higher social position than other shepherds, because the flocks in the city of the Nativity were destined to be used as sacrificial offerings in the Temple.

In the meadowland between Bethlehem and Jerusalem, a company of shepherds were keeping watch over their flocks on the memorable night of Jesus' birth. One writer states that that night the sky was almost like a miracle, so clear and so blue was it and filled with innumerable stars.

Suddenly the shepherds were enveloped in a glorious light, out of which came the voice of an angel telling them not to be afraid, for he brought them "good tidings of great joy."

The painting shows the shepherds' wonderment and awe. They move slowly up the hillside, one shepherd sinking to his knees, his shepherd's crook falling on the hem of his robe. Another shields his eyes against the blinding light; a third, bending on one knee, seems transfixed as he too hears the message.

Knowing the trepidation the shepherds must have felt, the angel of the Lord said, "Fear not: for, behold, I bring you good tidings of great joy, which shall be to all people. For unto you is born this day in the city of David a Saviour, which is Christ the Lord." At that moment, it seemed to the shepherds, "there was with the angel a multitude of the heavenly host praising God, and saying, Glory to God in the highest, and on earth peace, good will toward men."

The Scriptures continue the story of the shepherds in Luke 2:15 by telling us that after the angels had gone, they decided to "see this thing which is come to pass, which the Lord hath made known unto us."

THE SHEPHERDS ON THE HILLSIDE

And there were in the same country shepherds abiding in the field, keeping watch over their flock by night. And, lo, the angel of the Lord came upon them, and the glory of the Lord shone round about them: and they were sore afraid. And the angel said unto them, Fear not: for, behold, I bring you good tidings of great joy, which shall be to all people.

—Luke 2:8-10.

THE NATIVITY ❦ ❦ ❦ ❦ ❦ ❦ ❦ ❦

FOR nearly two thousand years the narrative of Jesus' birth, as told in Luke 2:1-20, has thrilled the heart of Christians no matter how often they have heard the story. Read aloud, it is probably one of the most moving and dramatic stories ever told, for no writer has ever excelled the lyric beauty of the Bible description. The Christmas story has been adapted and retold in many languages. The Nativity scene has also been glorified on canvas in scores of different versions, but regardless of the artist's conception its appeal is ever new.

In this painting the artist has departed somewhat from the traditional and has placed the Holy Family in an adjacent section of the cave-stable, rather than near the manger, where the oxen and cows were fed.

On a crude bench covered with a striped blanket, Mary sits and holds her Baby lovingly in her arms as she gazes down at Him with the adoration that only a mother can give her newborn child.

The artist has clothed the young mother in a pure white but simply cut robe, without any ornament such as adorned the garments of wealthy women, other than a band carrying out the same soft blue tones of her headdress.

It is apparent that Joseph is still awed by the divine birth, and so stands in a reverent and worshipful attitude beside Mary and the Infant Jesus.

Joseph's fur-trimmed cloak of dark brown affords a striking contrast to his purplish-blue tunic, and tends to bring Mary's simple garment into full focus.

In the far corner stands the little donkey, unmindful of the role he had played in carrying the young wife from Nazareth to Bethlehem.

The shepherds have arrived at the stable and wait at the entrance for the right moment to approach the Holy Family. We are told in Luke that after the angels had departed from the night sky, the shepherds went as quickly as they could to Bethlehem to find the young Child and His mother. No wonder they hastened, for as one writer says, "Joy quickened their steps."

We do not know whether the shepherds brought any gifts to the Baby Jesus, but it is certain that they brought deep and grateful love as they knelt before the Saviour, the promised King.

THE NATIVITY

For unto you is born this day in the city of
David a Saviour, which is Christ the Lord.

—Luke 2:11.

THE WISE MEN FOLLOW THE STAR

JOSEPH and Mary did not return to Nazareth immediately after the birth of the Saviour, but stayed for a while in Bethlehem. It was probably during this period that the three Wise Men from the East went to King Herod's palace in Jerusalem to inquire, "Where is he that is born King of the Jews? for we have seen his star in the east, and are come to worship him."

It is thought that these Magi had come from Babylon and were members of a priestly caste. In any event, it is quite likely they were astrologers and had been led by the strange phenomenon of the stars to make such a journey to Herod's palace.

King Herod was troubled when he heard the question of the Wise Men, for he felt his kingly power was in danger. So he called the chief priests and scribes to him and "demanded of them where Christ should be born."

The answer, "In Bethlehem of Judea: for thus it is written by the prophet," caused Herod to question the Wise Men closely about the time at which they had seen the star in the East. Then, without divulging the real purpose, he ordered them to go to Bethlehem to search diligently for the Child and to return so that he too might go to worship Him.

The Wise Men departed by night, to travel the five short miles from Jerusalem to Bethlehem. Mounted on their camels, they follow the star which they had seen in the East.

Early writers fix the number of the Magi as three and describe them as kings; the Bible, however, makes no mention of the number, nor of their names. Later legends call them Gaspar, Melchior, and Balthazar.

That the Magi possess considerable wealth is plainly shown in this painting in their costly embroidered robes, the trappings of their camels, and their retinue of servants.

As they ride, they follow the star, which goes before them. Here we see one of the kings pointing to the brilliant star, while the other two seem to be trying to shield their eyes from the brilliance of the heavens.

These lines fittingly express the hopes of the Wise Men as they search for the Messiah:

"We three kings of Orient are;
 Bearing gifts we traverse afar
 Field and fountain, moor and
   mountain,
 Following yonder star."

THE WISE MEN FOLLOW THE STAR

They departed; and, lo, the star, which
they saw in the east, went before them.

—*Matt. 2:9.*

THE WISE MEN PRESENT THEIR GIFTS

THE Gospel of Matthew is the only one of the Four Gospels that relates the visit of the Wise Men to the Holy Child.

It is supposed that by the time the Magi reached Bethlehem, Joseph had moved his little family from the cave-stable where Jesus had been born and had taken up temporary residence at a house in Bethlehem.

In such a home Mary and her little Baby would be more comfortable, so it was to this house that the Wise Men were directed by the star they had seen in the East. When the star hovered over the place, the three Wise Men dismounted from their camels, for they knew they had reached their destination.

Most Biblical authorities agree that the Magi arrived in Bethlehem twelve days after Christmas, and consequently in many Christian churches January 6 is celebrated as Twelfth Day or Epiphany.

Through the open doorway in this painting may be seen the star of Bethlehem as it hovers over the house. The camels rest outside, awaiting the return of their riders, while a herder watches over them to see that they do not stray.

Joseph, standing just inside the door, watches with intense interest the mother and Child seated on a rug on the stone floor. Since the room presumably was a temporary shelter for the Holy Family, there was little or no furniture.

The figures of the three Wise Men command attention. Two are kneeling in worship, while the third one seems bewildered by the beauty of the sleeping Child.

It was the custom in that part of the world to present gifts to important personages, and so the Wise Men bring to the Baby Jesus the most costly products of the country in which they lived — gold and frankincense and myrrh.

We are told that in the homage shown by the Magi, they understood that the Child before whom they knelt was the Messiah.

In Matt. 2:12 we learn that the Wise Men were warned in a dream that they should not return to Herod, who wanted to know where the Child was, so "they departed into their own country another way."

From the original painting in the George Washington Memorial Park, Inc., Whitemarsh, Pennsylvania.

THE WISE MEN PRESENT THEIR GIFTS

When they had opened their treasures, they presented unto him gifts; gold, and frankincense, and myrrh.

—*Matt. 2:11.*

THE RETURN TO NAZARETH

When Herod was dead, behold, an angel of the Lord appeareth in a dream to Joseph in Egypt,
Saying, Arise, and take the young child and his mother, and go into the land of Israel: . . .
And he arose, and took the young child and his mother, and came into the land of Israel.

—*Matt. 2:19-21.*

THE RETURN TO NAZARETH 🦢 🦢

OSEPH and Mary and the Baby Jesus stayed in safety in the land of Egypt during the remainder of the wicked King Herod's life. Soon after Herod's death, an angel of the Lord appeared to Joseph in a dream, saying, "Arise, and take the young child and his mother, and go into the land of Israel: for they are dead which sought the young child's life."

Joseph, however, knew that Herod's son now reigned, and he was afraid to return to that section of Judea.

One Biblical authority states that Joseph had intended to go to Bethlehem to live, but that he turned aside and took Mary and the Baby to Nazareth.

The caravan route from Egypt to Nazareth was about 250 miles—no mean distance to travel afoot or on donkeyback. We can well imagine how joyous the Holy Family must have been as they approached their old home in Nazareth just as the setting sun spread its glow over the valley.

A smile of contentment and happiness suffuses Mary's face, as Joseph points out to her the home in which they will live.

The donkey, the typical beast of burden in those days, carries Mary and the Baby Jesus, just as it had carried Mary into Bethlehem on the eve of the Saviour's birth.

THE BOY JESUS IN THE TEMPLE

T was the custom for the Jews of the land to go to Jerusalem to worship at the time of the Passover. Jesus' first visit to the Temple in Jerusalem was made when He was twelve years old.

For months Jesus had looked forward to seeing the Temple and, young as He was, His soul stirred as He listened to the words of the teachers in the courts so that, when it was time to go home to Nazareth, He stayed behind in the Temple.

At first Mary and Joseph did not miss the Boy, for there were many people in the caravan. But when night came and the Boy Jesus could not be found, His mother became alarmed. The next day she and Joseph hurried back to Jerusalem.

They searched for Jesus among their friends in the city, but they could not find Him. Finally, after looking for Him in vain for two days, they went to the Temple on the third day.

There they found Him sitting in one of the outer halls of the Temple in the midst of a group of teachers of the Law, listening to their words and asking questions.

The Gospel of Luke relates that when Mary approached the Boy and told Him that she and Joseph had been searching for Him, the Boy replied, "How is it that ye sought me? wist ye not that I must be about my Father's business?"

It is said that at that time Mary did not understand what Jesus meant, but that she thought about His reply often, for she realized that her Son was no ordinary child.

THE BOY JESUS IN THE TEMPLE

After three days they found him in the
temple, sitting in the midst of the doctors.

—*Luke 2:46.*

THE BAPTISM OF JESUS ➣ ➣ ➣ ➣

IT IS interesting to note that only one of the Four Gospels mentions the age of Jesus at the time of His baptism.

The Gospel of Luke tells us that when He came to the River Jordan to be baptized of John, He was about thirty years of age. It is supposed that He sought baptism partly because He approved of John the Baptist's work and also to prepare Himself for His own work on earth.

The Scriptures do not attempt to describe the method of baptism, but most of the old masters have depicted the scene with Jesus standing in the water and with John the Baptist, in somewhat the same manner as in this painting.

Few artists have depicted Jesus as shown here, His mature, manly form stripped to the waist, His arms outstretched, palms upward, as if to express His readiness to be about His "Father's business."

The soul-searching eyes and wistful expression seem to indicate that He is listening to the voice from heaven, saying, "Thou art my beloved Son; in thee I am well pleased."

The light above the Master's head is the artist's interpretation of the Holy Spirit of God that "descended on him like a dove."

Although Jesus is the central figure in the scene, the artist has furnished a picturesque background. John the Baptist, clad in a camel's-hair garment, having administered the rite of baptism, stands with clasped hands, awed by the presence of the Holy Spirit.

The blue waters of the Jordan eddy around Jesus' body as He comes "straightway out of the water," and the gnarled branches of a tree that fringe the River Jordan afford a bit of shade from the heat of the Palestinian day. Beneath the tree grows a cluster of anemones, which grew in abundance in Palestine.

In the distance between the trees on the opposite shore one can catch a glimpse of the sand dunes that are known to have bordered the river in that part of Palestine at the time of Jesus' life on earth.

THE BAPTISM OF JESUS

Jesus, when he was baptized, went up straightway out of the water.

—*Matt. 3:16.*

JESUS AND NICODEMUS ❧ ❧ ❧ ❧

THE story of Nicodemus is related only in the Gospel of John. In that book we are told that Nicodemus was a Pharisee and a member of the Sanhedrin, the supreme council and tribunal of the Jews.

At the time Jesus began his public ministry in Jerusalem, Nicodemus had occasion to hear Him, and he was much impressed with Jesus' teachings. He was convinced that Jesus was a teacher "come from God." His countrymen, though, were very much opposed to Jesus and His teachings.

For his own satisfaction Nicodemus sought an interview with Jesus. He chose the nighttime for his secret visit, possibly to avoid criticism from the other members of the Sanhedrin.

Tradition tells us that Jesus took His visitor to the housetop, where they could converse undisturbed. Here we see Jesus sitting in the soft glow of a light which, streaming through the window, forms a sort of halo about the Master's head. Nicodemus, in his rich and silken garments, sits in thoughtful contemplation, unmindful of the beauty of the star-filled sky over

the Holy City. He listens with close attention to Jesus' words.

Jesus has just explained to Nicodemus that unless a man be born again, he cannot enter the Kingdom of God. This statement bewilders Nicodemus, for he cannot understand how a man could be born again when he is already old.

Jesus then explains that one must be born of the Spirit, and that it was because of God's love for mankind that He sent His only-begotten Son into the world, so that "whosoever believeth in him should not perish, but have everlasting life."

Nicodemus left Jesus' presence that night as a true follower. He later defended Jesus at a meeting of the Sanhedrin when the members began to denounce Jesus and to accuse Him of being an impostor.

After the Crucifixion, Nicodemus, with Joseph of Arimathaea, another member of the Sanhedrin, aided in preparing Jesus' body for burial.

One Biblical authority relates that "in Nicodemus a noble candor and a simple love of truth shine out in the midst of hesitation and fear of man."

JESUS AND NICODEMUS

Nicodemus . . . came to Jesus by night.

—*John 3:1, 2.*

THE WOMAN OF SAMARIA ♘ ♘ ♘

ESUS has been traveling the hot, dusty road through Samaria on His way toward Galilee. Heat shimmers over the countryside behind Him, but here at Jacob's Well in the shade of an olive tree, Jesus has paused to rest.

The Samaritan woman who listens to the Master so intently has come to draw water. Deep in the cool shadow, her expression is one of rapt attention as she pauses in the act of lowering a vessel into the well. Jesus has asked for a drink of water. When the woman expresses surprise that He, a Jew, should even notice a Samaritan, whom the Jews despise as half pagan, He says to her, "If you would have asked me I would have given you living water."

So well has the artist captured this moment that it is not difficult to imagine the words being spoken. Even in the shade of the tree, a soft radiance surrounds the figure of Jesus, creating an effect of deep reverence.

This effect is skilfully heightened by the gleam of the white robe and by having the Samaritan woman's face and the upper portion of her figure cloaked in shadow. As a result, this artistic contrast between light and shade also serves to symbolize Christ's drawing of the woman toward the enlightenment of His wisdom, and His outstretched hand seems to possess a subtle power to attract and hold her attention.

"Sir," she ventures, "you have nothing to draw with. Where do you get that living water?"

After Jesus tells her, she says, "Sir, give me of that water that I may not thirst."

He speaks to her of her sinful life, and when she tells Him she knows the Messiah is coming, Jesus replies, "I who speak to you am He." Then she leaves Jesus as the disciples return. At the right of the picture we can see the disciples approaching. They seem to have paused in surprise at sight of the Master speaking to the woman of Samaria.

As they pause, the woman hurries to Sychar, telling the people about Jesus as she goes. Soon many profess their belief in Jesus, that He is indeed the Christ, the Saviour of the World.

From the original painting in the George Washington Memorial Park, Inc., Whitemarsh, Pennsylvania.

THE WOMAN OF SAMARIA

There cometh a woman of Samaria to draw
water: Jesus saith unto her, Give me to drink.

—*John 4:7.*

CALLING OF ANDREW AND PETER

Jesus said unto them, Come ye after me, and
I will make you to become fishers of men.

—*Mark 1:17.*

CALLING OF ANDREW AND PETER

ARLY in Jesus' ministry He began to choose His disciples, or followers, to accompany Him on His journeys and to assist Him in His preaching and healing missions. According to John 1:40, Andrew had been a disciple of John the Baptist and had already heard about Jesus, and had also told his brother, Simon Peter, about the Master.

Andrew and Peter were fishermen. One day as they were casting their nets near the shores of the Sea of Galilee, they saw Jesus coming toward them.

Many of the old masters have portrayed this scene by having the two men leave their nets and meet the Master on the shore. In this painting the artist has departed from the traditional and shows Jesus stepping into the water to greet the fishermen.

With outstretched hand, He approaches Andrew and Peter and says to them, "Follow me, and I will make you fishers of men." Andrew, seemingly a bit skeptical, still holds the net with a firm grip, but Peter, the impulsive one, the man of great strength, rises to full stature and confidently faces the Master, as if to say, "Here I am, take me."

As an example of His humility, Jesus was willing to go halfway to invite Andrew and Peter to join Him and to show the people that He needed the help of mankind to carry on His work on earth.

THE SERMON ON THE MOUNT

NE of the most exquisite passages in the Bible is the one that is known to Christians all over the world as the Sermon on the Mount. In it are included the Lord's Prayer, the Beatitudes, and the Golden Rule, as well as the familiar truths that explain the Master's conception of the Kingdom.

The Gospel of Matthew tells us that the Sermon on the Mount was delivered at the beginning of Jesus' Galilean ministry, supposedly on the flat-topped Horns of Hattin.

It was to this quiet mountaintop that Jesus retreated and to where great multitudes of people from Galilee and Decapolis and from beyond the Jordan followed Him.

When Jesus, who was resting on the mountain, saw the crowds, He called His disciples to Him. Grouped around Him on the left are James and John. On the right and slightly behind the Master are Peter, the stalwart disciple, and Thomas, the doubting one, with hand on chin.

In the foreground, a mother with her babe in arms sits with upturned face so that she can catch every word that Jesus speaks. Behind the Master, and grouped far down the hillside are the multitudes that have followed Jesus to hear Him preach.

Off in the distance, behind the pink Judas tree, can be seen the blue waters of the Sea of Galilee as it touches the slopes of the mountain. To further create a mood of beauty, the artist has drawn a cluster of anemones, the flower believed to be the lily of the field, growing by the water jar.

From the original painting in the George Washington Memorial Park, Inc., Whitemarsh, Pennsylvania.

THE SERMON ON THE MOUNT

And seeing the multitudes, he went up into a mountain: . . . And he opened his mouth, and taught them.

—*Matt. 5:1, 2.*

FEEDING OF THE FIVE THOUSAND

HE Gospel of Matthew tells us that immediately after Jesus had heard of the execution of John the Baptist, He called His disciples to Him, and they "departed thence by ship into a desert place apart."

On a hillside our Saviour continued to preach and to heal the throng of people who had followed Him, and there beside the Sea of Galilee the miracle of the loaves and fishes took place.

The rich green of the grass and the blueness of the waters of Galilee bordering the mountainside suggest that the event took place in late spring or early summer.

As the sun began to lower over the western hills, Jesus' disciples came to Him and reminded Him that the people were probably hungry. Jesus had been preaching and healing almost from early morning hours, and few if any of the people who had followed Him had brought food for their all-day outing.

We are told in the Scriptures that the disciples suggested to Jesus that the people be sent into the villages to buy food. Jesus' immediate reply, "Give ye them to eat," must have mystified the disciples, for they could not see how this could be done.

At that moment the lad with the basket of five loaves and two small fishes came up to Jesus. The artist has portrayed the incident with a satisfying richness of color.

The brilliant blue of the boy's garment, rivaling the color of the sea, is in striking contrast to the pure white robe of the Master. The setting sun throws a rich yellow glow over the Master's face and upper part of the body. All is suggestive of peace.

The Gospel story continues, with Jesus taking the bread and the fish from the boy after He had commanded the people to sit down in groups, as Christians have done down through the centuries. He gave thanks for the food and then broke the loaves and divided the two fishes. In the painting we see the wonder of the people near Him as they realize that something unusual is about to take place.

When all had eaten enough, Jesus told His disciples to gather up the pieces. Indeed, when they did gather up the fragments, these filled twelve baskets.

This miracle was one of the most marvelous the people had yet seen, and the Bible states that some of the men remarked, "This is of a truth that prophet that should come into the world."

From the original painting in the George Washington Memorial Park, Inc., Whitemarsh, Pennsylvania.

FEEDING OF THE FIVE THOUSAND

Jesus took the loaves; and when he had given thanks, he distributed to the disciples, and the disciples to them that were set down.

—John 6:11.

Two important events preceded the incident of this painting. John the Baptist had been sent to prison by King Herod and later beheaded to satisfy a whim of his daughter, Salome.

Jesus was sorely distressed when He learned that His cousin John had been put to death. Calling His disciples to Him, He departed with them by ship to a desert place on the other side of the Sea of Galilee. He had yet many works of mercy to do before He was to leave the world, but for a while He wanted to rest, with only His disciples to keep Him company.

Crowds of people followed Him, however, so when Jesus saw how eager the people were to hear Him, He felt compassion for them and taught them and healed those who were sick.

It was on this hillside that the miracle of the feeding of the five thousand took place, the second significant event of that period of Jesus' ministry.

After this miracle had been performed, Jesus sent the people away and told His disciples to go aboard a ship and row across the lake to Capernaum. Meanwhile, Jesus "went up into a mountain apart to pray: and when the evening was come, he was there alone."

The Gospels frequently mention Jesus' habit of prayer in conjunction with important events in His ministry, but as one authority states, "Prayer was also a part of Jesus' daily life."

How beautifully the artist has depicted this mountaintop experience of the Master! Even His garments take on the same hue as that of the setting sun, as the shadows "steal across the sky."

High on a mountaintop, the Master kneels with bowed head and clasped hands beside a huge boulder and prays, as He admonishes His followers to do, in secret, to His heavenly Father.

It is an interesting fact that clasping the hands in prayer, as the Saviour is shown doing, is the conventional form of holding up the hands toward heaven.

The earliest instance of this posture is found in Ex. 17:11, 12, where Aaron and Hur "stayed up" Moses' hands during a battle.

And like a heavenly benediction, the rays of the setting sun cast a golden light on His bowed head.

A PRAYER AT TWILIGHT

When he had sent the multitudes away, he went
up into a mountain apart to pray: and when
the evening was come, he was there alone.

—*Matt. 14:23*.

JESUS AND PETER ON THE WATER

HILE Jesus was praying alone and far into the night on the mountaintop, a violent storm arose on the Sea of Galilee. The wind was high and contrary, and the ship in which the disciples had set sail was being tossed about.

The disciples were very much afraid, for they realized that if the storm grew in intensity, they might all be drowned.

One Biblical authority states that Jesus could see the struggles of the boat and His disciples from the mountaintop, but that the men could not see Him. When the storm was at its worst, probably between three and six o'clock in the morning, the disciples were startled to see someone walking on the sea. At first the disciples thought the figure was a spirit, and they cried out in fear.

Straightway Jesus spoke to them, saying, "Be of good cheer; it is I; be not afraid." Peter, the spokesman for the Twelve, seemed to be in doubt that it was Jesus and said, "Lord, if it be thou, bid me come unto thee on the water."

The Master uttered but one word, "Come." Immediately Peter leaped onto the water, "But when he saw the wind boisterous," he lost his faith and began to sink. Then he cried out, "Lord, save me."

Just as Peter seems to be sinking beneath the huge waves swirling around him, the Saviour stretches out His hand and lifts Peter up. "O thou of little faith," He admonishes the disciple, "wherefore didst thou doubt?"

Five of the disciples meanwhile cling in desperate fear to the gunwale of the boat, as the waves dash high upon the starboard side.

They have abandoned their oars and seem to be waiting apprehensively for Peter to be rescued, for they as yet are not sure that Jesus is the Son of God.

Then we are told, in Matt. 14:32, that after Jesus led Peter safely to the ship, the wind ceased, and the sea became calm, and the men that were in the ship came and worshiped Jesus.

This miracle of walking on the water reveals that Jesus is truly the Son of God, and that He is always ready to give aid to His followers in time of temptation or trouble.

JESUS AND PETER ON THE WATER

Jesus stretched forth his hand, and caught him, and said unto him, O thou of little faith, wherefore didst thou doubt?

—*Matt 14:31.*

JESUS AT THE HOME OF
MARY AND MARTHA ❧ ❧ ❧ ❧ ❧ ❧

THE Gospels give us a few brief glimpses of times in Jesus' life when He visited homes of friends, where He was received with warm affection. On one occasion He visited the home of Mary and Martha and their brother Lazarus. Here at their little home in Bethany Jesus liked to tarry and to rest under the vine-covered trellis in the courtyard.

Mary, the younger of the two sisters, we are told, was eager to talk to the Master and to receive His instructions, while Martha kept busy in the role of housekeeper.

In this colorful painting of that scene, Mary sits at Jesus' feet and gazes up at Him with rapt attention. As He talks, He is shown raising His left hand in a gesture to emphasize some truth.

Mary, with clasped hands, seems oblivious of the approach of her more practical sister, whose countenance shows she is "cumbered about much serving."

Martha, however, is slow to understand her sister's more contemplative temperament, and she complains to Jesus. No doubt she is tired from her household duties, and she says, "Lord, dost thou not care that my sister hath left me to serve alone? bid her therefore that she help me."

The Master, who a moment before had been absorbed in talking to Mary, looks at Martha and admonishes her: "Martha, Martha, thou art careful and troubled about many things: but one thing is needful: and Mary hath chosen that good part, which shall not be taken away from her."

The lovely anemones, the abundance of grapes on the trellis, the fruit-laden tray carried by Martha, all indicate that the home of the two sisters and Lazarus was a home of beauty and plenty.

We are told in a well-known Bible dictionary that Martha's love, though imperfect in its form, is nevertheless recognized as being worthy; while Mary's love is that of a "contemplative believer."

"O Master, let me walk with Thee
In lowly paths of service free;
Tell me Thy secret; help me bear
The strain of toil, the fret of care."

JESUS AT THE HOME OF MARY AND MARTHA

Mary, . . . sat at Jesus' feet, and heard his word.

—Luke 10:39.

HEALING OF THE LEPER ❧ ❧ ❧

As Jesus made His way to Jerusalem, He preached and taught as He went. One day, as He passed through the midst of Samaria and Galilee, He came upon a certain small village. There He was met by ten men who stood a distance apart from Him. These men were lepers; and, because they were unclean, they were not permitted to mingle with other people.

The lepers stood off from Jesus and called loudly to Him, saying, "Master, have mercy on us."

Jesus, looking at the men with compassion, said, "Go shew yourselves unto the priests." As they turned and walked away from Jesus' presence, the dread disease left their bodies, and they were cleansed.

We are told that Jesus stood silently watching the men as they disappeared from view, before continuing on His way through the village.

As He was about to pass through one of the overhead arches in the street, He was arrested by the sound of running footsteps.

We know from the Bible story of the cleansing of the lepers, in Luke, chapter 17, that Jesus fully expected the ten to return to express their gratitude to Him for healing them.

But only one of the ten returned, and he was a Samaritan. Here we see the man on his knees at Jesus' feet, thanking Him for cleansing him of his leprosy. His lowly position and his countenance show that he is grateful for what the Master has done for him.

He, the Samaritan, was the only one of the ten who were healed who had not forgotten to thank God for His mercies.

The Master, though inquiring about the other nine, gave His blessing to the Samaritan and told him to "Arise, go thy way: thy faith hath made thee whole."

It should be noted that in healing leprosy Jesus not only laid stress on the actual healing act but also on the ceremonial cleansing which restored a person to his rightful position in society.

In the dramatic story of the ten lepers, there is a lesson for all of us. How many of us remember to thank God for his goodness to us?

"Giving thanks always for all things unto God and the Father in the name of our Lord Jesus Christ."

HEALING OF THE LEPER

Jesus, moved with compassion, put forth his hand, and touched him, and saith unto him, . . . be thou clean. And as soon as he had spoken, immediately the leprosy departed from him, and he was cleansed.

—*Mark 1:41, 42.*

RAISING OF LAZARUS

He cried with a loud voice, Lazarus, come
forth. And he that was dead came forth.

—John 11:43, 44.

RAISING OF LAZARUS ﺔﻟ ﺔﻟ ﺔﻟ ﺔﻟ

As Jesus journeyed toward Jerusalem, a messenger came to Him with the report that Lazarus, the brother of Mary and Martha, was very ill.

The messenger was given a comforting reply to carry back to the sisters in Bethany, "This sickness is not unto death, but for the glory of God."

Jesus did not go at once to Bethany, and in the meantime Lazarus had died. Four days after Lazarus had been buried, Jesus and the Twelve arrived in Bethany.

When Martha heard that Jesus was approaching, she went to meet Him, but Mary stayed in the house. When Mary heard that Jesus had asked for her, she hurried to Him and cried out, "Lord, if thou hadst been here, my brother had not died."

In utmost tenderness, Jesus looked at her and, although we are not told what the Master said, we do know that He revealed His tender sympathy. "Jesus wept." This is the shortest verse in the Bible and yet one of the most revealing of the Saviour's love for mankind.

"Where have ye laid him?" Jesus then asked. Mary and Martha answered, "Lord, come and see."

The Saviour bade those around the cave-tomb to roll away the stone that covered the entrance. Martha, who believed in the power of her Lord, hardly dared to think He would show Himself to be the Son of God then and there.

Jesus reproved Martha by saying, "If thou wouldest believe, thou shouldest see the glory of God." With that, He lifted up His eyes and cried aloud, "Lazarus, come forth."

THE GOOD SAMARITAN ﺔﻟ ﺔﻟ ﺔﻟ ﺔﻟ

The Parable of the Good Samaritan is recorded only in the Gospel of Luke.

On one occasion when Jesus was asked by a scribe seeking to have eternal life, "Who is my neighbor?" He answered by telling the story of a man traveling from Jerusalem to Jericho who was set upon by thieves, who stripped him of his goods and clothing and then wounded him, leaving him half dead.

Later a certain priest came down that same road and saw the man lying there. But the priest did not stop. He continued on his way, passing by on the other side. Some time later a Levite also came down the road, but he too passed by on the other side.

Then a Samaritan happened along. As shown in the painting, he stopped to give the man succor. He poured oil and wine on his wounds and bound them.

Then he helped the wounded man onto his own beast of burden and took him to an inn, where he took care of the traveler all through the night. In the morning the Samaritan gave the landlord money, saying, "Whatsoever thou spendest more, when I come again, I will repay thee." He did all this even though he knew that as a Samaritan he was considered an enemy by the man. By this parable Jesus shows that "our neighbor" is anyone who needs our help, even our enemies.

THE GOOD SAMARITAN

A certain Samaritan, as he journeyed, came where he was: and when he saw him, he had compassion on him.

—*Luke 10:33*.

JESUS BLESSES CHILDREN ❧ ❧ ❧

Three of the Gospels, Matthew, Mark, and Luke, tell the story of Jesus blessing little children. Jesus undoubtedly was happier when He was surrounded with children than at any other time. He loved them, and of course they loved Him.

Those of the disciples who were with Jesus on such occasions were annoyed when parents brought their little ones to the Master. They tried to turn the children aside, for they did not like to see Jesus interrupted. Jesus, however, rebuked His disciples, saying to them, "Suffer little children, and forbid them not, to come unto me: for of such is the kingdom of heaven."

Few artists have been successful in bringing out the joy in Jesus' face as has been done in this painting of the Master with a little child on His lap.

Jesus and His disciples had been traveling through Perea toward Jerusalem when this touching incident took place.

So many children had been brought to Him that He stopped in a vine-covered courtyard and sat down on a large stone so that the children could come close to Him.

The older children cluster around Him, their faces alight with pleasure because of their nearness to the Saviour. Several of them have brought flowers to Jesus, and even the little girl on His lap offers Him a single blossom of the anemone. These flowers flourished in Biblical times and supposedly were the "lilies of the field" referred to in the Bible.

A father and a mother, each carrying a baby, approach Jesus eagerly so that they too might receive a blessing for their children.

Even the two disciples standing in the background seem to be watching the scene with interest, as if they have come to the realization that Christ's recognition of little children was an important phase of His ministry.

"I wish that His hands had been placed
 on my head,
 That His arm had been thrown
  around me,
 And that I might have seen His kind
  look when He said,
 'Let the little ones come unto Me.'"

JESUS BLESSES CHILDREN

Suffer the little children to come unto me, and forbid them not: for of such is the kingdom of God.

—*Mark 10:14.*

ZACCHAEUS, THE PUBLICAN ໒∾ ໒∾

As Jesus passed through Jericho, great multitudes followed Him to see Him and to hear Him preach. Among the crowd was a publican whose name was Zacchaeus.

The publicans were the tax collectors of that time and, as such, were looked upon by the people as little better than thieves and even as traitors to their own people.

Despite his occupation, Zacchaeus had an intense desire to see the One who could attract crowds of people.

Zacchaeus was short of stature, however, and was unable to see Jesus above the heads of the throng. So he ran ahead of the crowd and climbed up into a sycomore tree to wait until Jesus would come abreast of him.

The sycomore tree mentioned in the Bible is supposed to have been really a mulberry tree. It grows by the wayside, and its giant branches stretch across the roadway. Just as the painting shows, it was easy for Zacchaeus to climb this tree and look directly down on the crowd passing beneath. It was admirably adapted to the use for which Zacchaeus selected it.

The painting shows the Master as He approached the tree. Both grownups and children gathered around Him as He raised His hand to greet the little tax collector.

"Zacchaeus, make haste," He called, "and come down; for today I must abide at thy house." For Jesus to be willing to visit the home of a despised publican surprised the onlookers, and they began to murmur among themselves, for they considered Zacchaeus a sinner.

How did Jesus know this man's name? Why did He choose him as His host? Certainly, Zacchaeus could not tell, but we do know he was touched by Jesus' words, and he hurried down out of the tree. The Bible tells us that he "received him joyfully."

The little, once-despised publican gave up half of his wealth to the poor and promised to make restitution for his misdeeds.

The Master recognized Zacchaeus' sincerity, and He knew also that Zacchaeus was ready to receive Him as his Saviour, so He said, "This day is salvation come to this house, forsomuch as he also is a son of Abraham."

ZACCHAEUS THE PUBLICAN

He sought to see Jesus . . . and could not for the press, because he was little of stature. And he ran before, and climbed into a sycomore tree.

—Luke 19:3, 4.

JESUS LAMENTS OVER JERUSALEM

AFTER Jesus had driven the moneychangers from the Temple in Jerusalem, He went out of the city into Bethany, lodged there overnight, returning to the Holy City in the morning.

There He continued His teaching, speaking in parables. It was at this time that He explained to the Pharisees the meaning of the Great Commandment of the Law, "Thou shalt love the Lord thy God with all thy heart, and with all thy soul, and with all thy mind. This is the first and great commandment. And the second is like unto it. Thou shalt love thy neighbor as thyself. On these two commandments hang all the law and the prophets."

Jesus likewise rebuked the scribes and Pharisees for their hypocritical ways and denounced them as whited sepulchers, and described them as a "generation of vipers," upon whom all manner of destruction would most assuredly come.

Mark states that following the denunciation of the scribes and Pharisees, Jesus went out to the Mount of Olives and lamented over the Holy City. The artist vividly portrays this scene of the Master looking down over the fair city of Jerusalem from a lofty height above the city. His disciples accompanied Him, but the artist shows only Peter and James and John and Andrew grouped behind Him as He gazes sadly down at Jerusalem.

The younger man, with chin on hand, is the beloved John; the tall, bearded, powerful one, his gaze fixed also on the city below, could very well be Simon Peter.

Giving vent to His sorrow, Christ cries out, "O Jerusalem, Jerusalem, thou that killest the prophets, and stonest them which are sent unto thee, how often would I have gathered thy children together, even as a hen gathereth her chickens under her wings, and ye would not! Behold, your house is left unto you desolate. For I say unto you, Ye shall not see me henceforth, till ye shall say, Blessed is he that cometh in the name of the Lord."

Maunder's oratorio "Olivet to Calvary," describes Jerusalem as "a diadem on Zion's holy hill," on which Jesus gazed with "tearful eyes."

No doubt He was thinking of another procession in those same streets of Jerusalem when the people would be shouting "Crucify him" instead of shouting His praises.

JESUS LAMENTS OVER JERUSALEM

O Jerusalem, Jerusalem, . . . how often would I have gathered thy children together, even as a hen gathereth her chickens under her wings, and ye would not!

—*Matt. 23:37.*

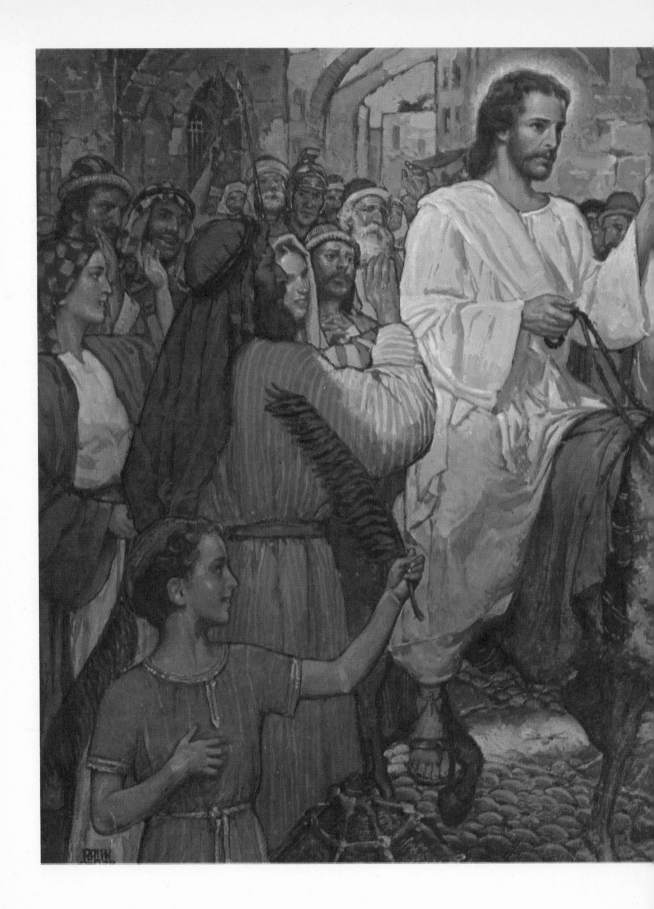

JESUS ENTERS JERUSALEM

And many spread their garments in the way: and others cut down branches off the trees, and strawed them in the way. And they that went before, and they that followed, cried, saying, Hosanna; Blessed is he that cometh in the name of the Lord.

—*Mark 11:8, 9.*

JESUS ENTERS JERUSALEM ❧ ❧ ❧ ❧

I
N the first day of the last week of Jesus' life, He triumphantly entered Jerusalem. One Biblical authority refers to the entry into Jerusalem as "the one gleam of light in the dark days that closed our Lord's ministry."

Our Saviour had prepared for it by sending two of His disciples from Bethphage into a neighboring village to find an ass and a colt and to bring them to Him.

It is an interesting fact that Matthew alone mentions the two animals. Our Saviour rode only the ass, as it was the symbol of humility and peace.

As the procession made its way through the gate into the Holy City, many of the people spread their garments in the way, an extraordinary token of respect usually paid to kings and conquerors.

Jesus became surrounded by a multitude of cheering, joyous people. Beside themselves with excitement, they tore down branches of the palm trees and waved them before Him.

As the crowd grew in numbers, the shouts of "Hosanna! Hosanna!" increased in volume. "Hosanna to the son of David," they cried. "Blessed is he that cometh in the name of the Lord; Hosanna in the highest."

The Gospel of Luke adds to Mark's account of the triumphal entry by relating that some of the Pharisees who were watching the procession asked Jesus to rebuke the disciples for rejoicing and praising God.

Jesus answered them, saying, "If these should hold their place, the stones would immediately cry out."

This picture portrays that moment when the crowd was densest, and when a shaft of sunlight bathed the figure of Christ in a radiant glow.

Thus we see Jesus "in lowly pomp" riding on to die, on that memorable day that is celebrated as Palm Sunday, in remembrance of the way the cheering throngs honored Christ, the Son of David.

When He entered the city, with the multitude that followed Him, the people were filled with wonder. They asked, "Who is this?" and Matthew tells us the multitude replied, "This is Jesus the prophet of Nazareth of Galilee."

CLEANSING THE TEMPLE &ref; &ref; &ref;

THE first Palm Sunday ended with Jesus and His disciples going back over the road along which He had made His triumphal entry. That night He lodged in Bethany, and early Monday morning He returned to Jerusalem, going first to the Temple.

The scene that He came upon as He entered the Court of the Gentiles filled Him with wrath. He saw it filled with traders and their wares, men who were changing the money for use in the Temple, and others selling the doves customarily used for sacrifices.

The laughter and shouting and bickering of the mob upset the Master, for He knew that the noise disturbed the worship in the Temple itself. He was indignant that these traders were profaning the house of God. Stepping into the midst of the crowd, and picking up a whip, or double-headed strap of cowhide, Jesus exclaimed, "My house shall be called the house of prayer; but ye have made it a den of thieves."

We can imagine the consternation of the people as Jesus began to drive out the traders.

The priests and the Pharisees and all the scribes who were guilty of permitting the Father's house to become a place of trading and selling dared not prevent Jesus, for they knew that such acts were illegal. Yet they knew, as Jesus knew, and as one historian states, that this act was bringing the death of the Man of Galilee closer.

The artist has created the commotion caused by Jesus' action both picturesquely and dramatically. Even a greedy look shows on the faces of the hagglers as they try to gather up their scattered coins and pick up the broken cages in which the doves of the Temple were kept.

The moneychanger standing directly in front of Jesus seems to be denouncing Him, and at the same time he clutches his moneybag close to his person.

The trader clasping the dove cage seems frightened, as if he expected someone to steal his booty, while others craftily scoop up as many coins as possible.

And yet, despite the commotion, the crowd seems overawed by the presence of the stern and mighty Master.

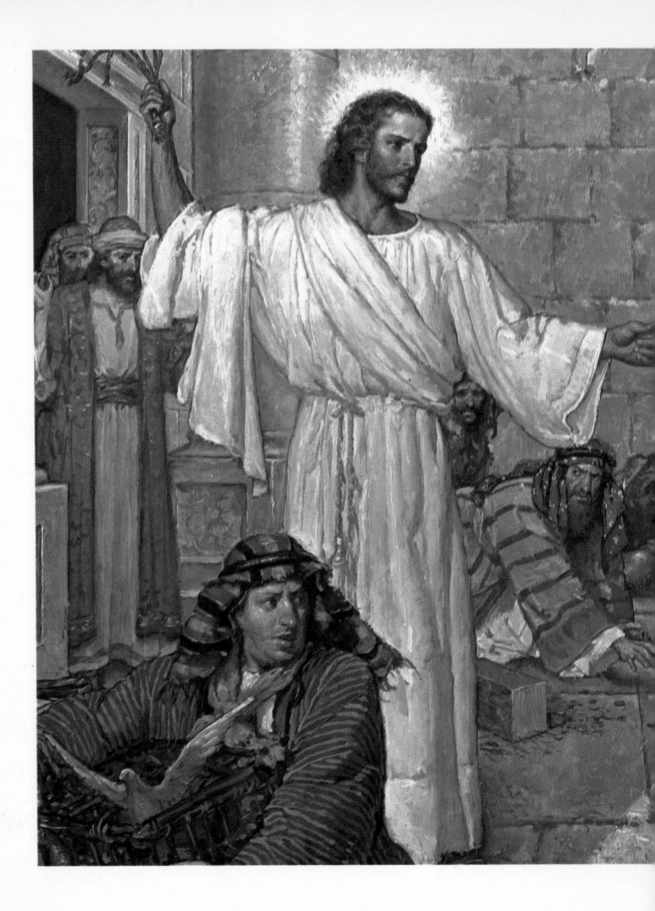

CLEANSING THE TEMPLE

And they come to Jerusalem: and Jesus went into the temple, and began to cast out them that sold and bought in the temple, and overthrew the tables of the moneychangers, . . . And he taught, saying unto them, Is it not written, My house shall be called of all nations the house of prayer? but ye have made it a den of thieves.

—*Mark 11:15-17.*

PERHAPS the most famous picturization of Jesus' last night on earth when He instituted the Lord's Supper is Leonardo da Vinci's painting which has for centuries been seen by throngs of people in the convent church of Santa Maria delle Gracie in Milan, Italy. Even in its present state of deterioration, it is still one of the world's art masterpieces, and many artists have depicted the scene in similar manner.

In this painting of the Last Supper, however, the composition is arranged vertically rather than in the traditional horizontal form. The artist has shown remarkable skill in grouping the disciples, with the surface of the table serving as an optical pathway to the central figure of Christ. Around the gleaming cloth the disciples are shown in attitudes that draw attention to the head of the table. Even Judas, who has turned his face from the Master, is so placed that the line of his arm, with the elbow resting on the table, leads to the inevitable center of interest while Judas himself becomes a secondary focal point.

Jesus in His pure white robe stands at His rightful place at the head of the table. Behind Him, through the arched openings in the upper room, the star-lit sky over the city of Jerusalem forms a fitting background for the scene.

Around the table are seated the disciples, Peter on the left of Jesus, and John the beloved disciple on His right. Next to John, Judas the betrayer grips the table as he turns his face away from Jesus.

Jesus and His disciples have just been keeping the Passover. He startles the disciples as He says, "Verily I say unto you, One of you which eateth with me shall betray me." The disciples become very sorrowful and ask, "Is it I?" Jesus tells them that it will be one of the Twelve who eat with Him.

Jesus speaks to Judas, saying, "What thou doest, do quickly."

The disciples apparently do not realize what Jesus means by that remark, for they know that Judas has been entrusted with their moneybag, and they suppose He is telling him to lose no time in buying the things for which they have need.

Then the Saviour takes the bread and blesses it and gives it to His disciples, saying, "Take, eat; this is my body." He then lifts the cup, saying, "This is my blood of the new testament, Drink ye all of it."

The Bible tells us that after these events, they sang a hymn and went out into the Mount of Olives.

THE LORD'S SUPPER

Jesus took bread, and blessed, and brake it, and gave to them, and said, Take, eat: this is my body. And he took the cup, and when he had given thanks, he gave it to them: and they all drank of it.

—*Mark 14:22, 23.*

CHRIST IN GETHSEMANE ❧ ❧ ❧

AFTER leaving the upper room where the Last Supper had been celebrated, Jesus and eleven of His disciples crossed the brook Kidron into the Garden of Gethsemane. The Garden lay in a secluded hollow on the western slope of the Mount of Olives and was well-known to the disciples as a place where Jesus often went to pray.

As Jesus and the disciples drew near, Jesus said to them, "Sit ye here, while I go and pray yonder."

He took with Him three chosen disciples, Peter, James, and John, the three who had witnessed His Transfiguration. The others sat under the trees, while Jesus and Peter and James and John advanced farther into the Garden.

Turning to the three disciples, Jesus said, "My soul is exceeding sorrowful, even unto death: tarry ye here, and watch with me."

He then went forward alone and, as we see Him in this painting, fell to His knees beside a large rock, His hands clasped in prayer, His face upturned toward heaven.

A brilliant light from above shines over the Master's head, and the entire figure of Jesus is bathed in that holy light in the otherwise dark and secluded garden. The beautiful anemones at the Master's feet seem to lift their heads so that they too may draw close to the sanctity of His being.

The look on Jesus' face shows that He knew that His hour was drawing near, that He could expect His enemies that night. His anguish of soul found expression in the words, "O my Father, if it be possible, let this cup pass from me: nevertheless not as I will, but as thou wilt."

The twenty-sixth chapter of Matthew relates that three times during Jesus' agony in the Garden He appealed to His three chosen disciples for sympathy, but each time He found them sleeping. Even Peter failed Him. And to him we find Jesus saying, "Could ye not watch with me one hour?"

At last Jesus rose from prayer and said to His disciples, "Sleep on now, and take your rest: . . . behold, he is at hand that doth betray me."

His startled companions rose hastily. But Jesus did not now need their watchful care. It was too late, for Judas, the traitor, was approaching.

" 'Tis midnight; and on Olive's brow
The star is dimmed that lately shone:
'Tis midnight; in the garden now,
The suffering Saviour prays alone."

CHRIST IN GETHSEMANE

He went forward a little, and fell on the ground, and prayed that, if it were possible, the hour might pass from him. And he said, Abba, Father, all things are possible unto thee; take away this cup from me: nevertheless not what I will, but what thou wilt.

—Mark 14:35, 36.

THE BETRAYAL OF JESUS ✣ ✣ ✣

ITH lighted torches and the betrayer to show them the way, the company of soldiers, guards, and servants, and even some priests whom Judas had incited to action, neared in the darkness on Gethsemane.

As Jesus emerged from the Garden of Gethsemane where He had been praying to His Father to give Him strength to face suffering and death, He saw a flicker of lights in the distance. He heard the sound of men's voices advancing toward Him through the gloom.

He knew that His hour had now come, that Judas was approaching. Jesus knew that Judas had turned traitor and that he had offered to betray Him to the chief priests for a price.

The priests and Judas had mutually agreed on thirty pieces of silver, an ordinary price for a slave. They had also arranged a sign. Whomever Judas kissed, he was the one the soldiers were to seize.

In this painting we get a vivid picture of that dramatic moment. Judas is seen standing to the rear of Jesus. He lacks the courage to face the Master, and his countenance shows the avarice and covetousness that lurk in his traitor's heart.

Jesus, meanwhile, stands calmly and regally with clasped hands, awaiting the deceitful kiss. Excitement spreads through the unruly crowd as they press forward to seize Jesus. Peter, the impulsive one, has drawn his sword. As the Bible relates in Matt. 26:51, he struck at one of the men in the front of the mob and cut off his right ear. Tradition tells us that this man was a servant of the high priest and that his name was Malchus.

The Bible story continues with Jesus turning to Peter and saying, "Put up again thy sword into his place: for all they that take the sword shall perish with the sword."

Following this admonition to Peter, Jesus turned to the multitude and said, "Are ye come out as against a thief with swords and staves for to take me? I sat daily with you in the temple, and ye laid no hold on me."

With this the leaders of the mob rushed forward and bound Jesus and then led Him away to Caiaphas, the high priest.

The disciples, whom we would have expected to protect Jesus, left Him alone with His enemies. They all "forsook him, and fled."

THE BETRAYAL OF JESUS

Judas, one of the twelve, came, . . . to
Jesus, and said, Hail, master; and kissed him.

—Matt. 26:47, 49.

THE enemies of Jesus had led Him away, bound, to the house of Caiaphas, the high priest. Their purpose was to have witnesses testify before the chief priests that Jesus had said wicked things. If it could be proved that He had, then, according to the Mosaic Law, He could be put to death.

There were none, however, who could truthfully testify against Jesus, so false witnesses were hired for that purpose. They declared that Jesus had said that He would destroy the Temple and rebuild it in three days.

Caiaphas then turned to Jesus, inquiring whether He denied this charge. Jesus did not answer.

The high priest was not satisfied. He wanted Jesus to condemn Himself. He then asked Him, "Are you the Son of God?" The Master's direct answer, "I am," was the answer Caiaphas desired, and he immediately accused Jesus of blasphemy.

As Jesus was led away, hands bound together with stout cords, a familiar voice reached His ears. It was that of His disciple and friend, Simon Peter.

Peter had followed Jesus to the high priest's house. There he had mingled with the gathering crowd in the courtyard, hoping that he would not be noticed. But a servant who heard his voice and recognized him, accused him of being a follower of Jesus. Peter denied it, saying, "Woman, I know him not."

A little later another woman servant saw Peter and said, "This man was one of those with Jesus." A second time Peter denied his Master.

Soon a man came by, looked at Peter, and said, "You are one of this man's disciples, for by your speech I can tell you came from Galilee."

For the third time, Peter denied knowing Jesus, by saying, "Man, I know not what thou sayest."

Just then the loud, shrill crowing of a cock startled Peter. It was then that he looked up and saw Jesus.

In this scene we see Jesus as He gazes down at Peter, a soft light illuminating His face. Peter is outlined by the glow of the fire which the people had started to warm themselves as they waited to hear about Jesus' trial.

But it is not a look of compassion on Peter's face; it is a look of remorse, as he attempts to hide behind the pillar. As the eyes of Master and disciple meet, there flashes into Peter's mind what Jesus had said the previous evening. "Before the cock crow, thou shalt deny me thrice."

Peter, with despair in his heart, "went out, and wept bitterly," because he had denied his Lord.

PETER'S DENIAL

The Lord turned, and looked upon Peter. And Peter remembered the word of the Lord, how he had said unto him, Before the cock crow, thou shalt deny me thrice.

—Luke 22:61.

CHRIST BEFORE PILATE

Then came Jesus forth, wearing the crown of thorns, and the purple robe.
And Pilate saith unto them, Behold the man! When the chief priests therefore and officers saw him, they cried out, saying, Crucify him, crucify him.

—John 19:5, 6.

CHRIST BEFORE PILATE ໃ ໃ ໃ ໃ

UFFERED under Pontius Pilate." Through the ages this phrase has been repeated wherever the story of Christ has been told. There have been many conceptions both in art and literature of this memorable scene when Jesus was led as a condemned man to Pontius Pilate, the Roman governor, but few depict the drama of the event as in this painting.

Clad in purple robe, His wrists bound with iron bands, and with a crown of thorns about His head, the royal prisoner stands guarded by two Roman soldiers as Pilate addresses the crowd in the street.

One of the armor-clad soldiers holds aloft a staff bearing the letters *S.P.Q.R.,* signifying in English, the "Senate and People of Rome."

The guard behind the Saviour, with spear poised, seems ready if necessary to prevent any untoward movement on the part of his prisoner.

In the entrance, Claudia, the wife of Pilate, stands with downcast eyes as if reluctant to witness the unjust treatment of Jesus. It was she who warned her husband, "Have thou nothing to do with that just man: for I have suffered many things this day in a dream because of him."

Between Claudia and the Roman soldier may be seen the basin in which Pilate washed his hands before the multitude and claimed that he was innocent of the blood of Jesus.

When the mob shout that Barabbas should be released, Pilate in disappointment, scorn, and anger points to his prisoner and shouts, "What shall I do then with Jesus which is called Christ?"

"Crucify him, crucify him!" the people shout. Even though Jesus had admitted He was the King of the Jews, Pilate still could find no fault in Him. However, Pilate could see the faces of the mob clouding with anger and excitement growing, so he yielded to their cries, and "delivered him to be crucified."

The pageantry of this scene brings to focus the godlike calmness and majestic dignity of the Saviour as He goes forth to die for the salvation of His people.

CHRIST ON THE CROSS ❧ ❧ ❧ ❧

THE portrayal of the Crucifixion has taken many forms in artists' minds since that dark Friday in A.D. 30, when our Saviour was nailed to the cross.

One of the most famous paintings of the scene is by Munkácsy, a celebrated Hungarian artist of the nineteenth century. He, like the other masters, emphasized Christ's suffering by showing the entire figure on the cross.

In this painting only the lower portion of our Saviour's body is shown, His feet nailed to a support, thus suggesting rather than emphasizing His agony.

Alongside the cross, on the grassy slope of Golgotha, may be seen the basin of vinegar and the sponge, which had been raised to the lips of the dying Jesus. The mallet used to drive the huge nails into the Master's hands and feet, and the spade, used to dig the hole for the cross, supply details not portrayed by other artists.

Among the people gathered around the cross, Mary, the mother of Jesus, commands attention as she gazes up-ward into the face of her dying Son. Filled with sorrow though she was, she stands bravely and dry-eyed before the cross of the One she had taken as an infant to the Temple more than thirty years earlier.

But Mary in her grief does not stand alone. John, the beloved disciple, supports her tenderly as he promises the dying Jesus to take her into his care.

The Roman centurion in the foreground, who had been charged with the execution of the death warrant, was so moved by the sublime dignity of Christ on the cross that he exclaimed, "Truly this was the Son of God." The other centurion, however, remains indifferent and arrogant.

The figure in the distance below the second centurion is Mary Magdalene, who, unable to bear the terrible sight, stands with head bowed and eyes covered.

Over the entire scene a strange darkness descended, until Jesus spoke His last words on the cross: "Father, into thy hands I commend my spirit."

And Luke adds, "Having said thus, he gave up the ghost."

CHRIST ON THE CROSS

When Jesus therefore saw his mother, and the disciple standing by, whom he loved, he saith unto his mother, Woman, behold thy son! Then saith he to the disciple, Behold thy mother! And from that hour that disciple took her unto his own home.

—*John 19:26, 27.*

JESUS APPEARS TO MARY MAGDALENE

ARY Magdalene, who had witnessed the Crucifixion from afar and who had returned to the sepulcher where Jesus had been buried, was the first person, according to John's Gospel, to whom the risen Lord manifested Himself.

On that first Easter morning, Mary went early to the sepulcher before the sun was up, and as she drew near the tomb she was startled to see that the stone from the door of the sepulcher had been rolled away.

Her joy was turned to sadness in her discovery that the tomb was empty, for "the Lord she loved was gone."

The Gospel of Matthew refers to another Mary, the wife of Cleophas, as having accompanied Mary Magdalene to the tomb, but John mentions only the one Mary.

It was she, we are told, who ran to report her discovery of the empty tomb to Peter and "to the other disciple, whom Jesus loved."

Peter and John, determining to know the truth of Mary's story, hurried to the tomb. John outran Peter, but being too timid to enter, he waited for Peter to arrive. When Peter reached the sepulcher, he went in, and John followed him.

There lay the graveclothes in perfect order; the napkin which had been about His head had been "wrapped together in a place by itself."

When John saw the clothes, but not Jesus' body, he believed that Jesus had risen; while Peter, we are told, "marveled yet more" as the two disciples returned to their homes.

Mary Magdalene, however, lingered at the tomb after Peter and John had departed. She stood outside the tomb weeping, for she feared that Jesus' enemies had taken away His body.

As Jesus had wept at the grave of Lazarus, she wept at His. Still weeping, she looked in the tomb and saw "two angels in white sitting, the one at the head, and the other at the feet, where the body of Jesus had lain."

They spoke to her, saying, "Woman, why weepest thou?" Mary answered that they had taken away her Lord.

At that moment a Figure bathed in a dazzling light stood before her, and a voice said, "Woman, why weepest thou?" So unexpected was the appearance of Jesus that Mary did not recognize Him at first and supposed that He was the gardener. Hardly looking at Him, she begged Him to tell her where Jesus' body had been laid.

Then Jesus said to her, "Mary," and in that instant she recognized her Master.

JESUS APPEARS TO MARY MAGDALENE

Now when Jesus was risen early the first day
of the week, he appeared first to Mary Magdalene, out of whom he had cast seven devils.

—Mark 16:9.

THE WOMEN AT THE TOMB ❧ ❧

ON that first Easter morning, even before daybreak, three women, carrying ointment and spices to anoint and embalm the body of Jesus, hastened from their homes through the streets of the still sleeping city to the garden tomb.

The Gospel of Mark names these women as Mary Magdalene, Mary the mother of James, and Salome.

As they approached the sepulcher, the women asked themselves who was to roll away the stone from the door, "for it was very great."

When they reached the entrance, they saw that the seal had been broken, that the stone had been rolled away, and that the Roman soldiers who had guarded the tomb were gone.

They did not know that before they came to the sepulcher there had been an earthquake, Matt. 28:2, and that an angel had rolled back the stone.

Mary Magdalene, the first to enter the tomb, was followed by Salome. And last came the oldest of the three, Mary, the mother of James.

Awed by the dazzling light that shone from the place where Jesus had lain, Mary Magdalene falls to her knees and clasps her hands in wonder. Salome, the box of spices still firmly grasped in her left hand, seems filled with fear, as she too gazes in wonder-

ment at the glow surrounding the angel, unseen in this artist's portrayal of the Resurrection.

Mary, the mother of James, seems calmer than the other two as she stands erect just inside the opening. All of them appear troubled, for the angel now speaks, saying, "Fear not ye: for I know that ye seek Jesus, which was crucified. He is not here: for he is risen, as he said. Come, see the place where the Lord lay." Matt. 28: 5, 6. Then he commands them to go quickly and tell His disciples that the Lord is risen from the dead.

In this painting there are shown several impressive details.

On the slab over which the grave-cloth had been laid, the artist has placed the crown of thorns as a reminder of Christ's suffering and agony on the cross.

Just inside the entrance, a shield lies forgotten, as if it had been dropped in haste by one of the Roman soldiers who had guarded the tomb as he fled from the presence of the risen Lord.

In the background may be seen the three crosses silhouetted against the early morning light as they rise above the skull-like formation of Golgotha, whence the name was derived.

The Resurrection of Christ from the dead on Easter Day is the very essence of the Christian religion.

THE WOMEN AT THE TOMB

They entered in, and found not the body of the Lord Jesus.

—*Luke 24:3.*

THE ASCENSION &~ &~ &~ &~ &~ &~ &~

ORTY days after the Resurrection, the eleven disciples "went away into Galilee, into a mountain where Jesus had appointed them." The Gospel of Luke states that this mountain was near Bethany, a place to which the Master and His disciples had often gone.

Suddenly the disciples saw Jesus standing in their midst. Falling upon their knees, they knelt on the ground and worshiped Him.

Jesus spoke unto them, Matt. 28:19 relates, saying, "Go ye therefore, and teach all nations, baptizing them in the name of the Father, and of the Son, and of the Holy Ghost."

With those words, Jesus lifted up His hands, and blessed the Eleven, and while He was blessing them, He was parted from them and carried up into heaven, until a cloud made it impossible for them to see Him any more.

In this scene, the majority of the Eleven seemed startled and overwhelmed by the sight of Jesus being carried up into heaven. A few, however, seemed to doubt that this miraculous disappearance of Jesus was possible. The artist has pictured this skepticism very plainly on the face of the fourth disciple, and likewise on the countenance of the one stroking his beard.

There is an ethereal quality about this painting as the Saviour, hands upraised toward heaven, rises from the snowy bank of clouds into the azure blue of the heavens.

In Luke 24:51 we are told that, "when it came to pass, while he blessed them, he was parted from them, and carried up into heaven."

The Gospel of Mark adds to the record of the Ascension by stating that after He was received up into heaven, He "sat on the right hand of God."

The disciples, after witnessing the Ascension, returned joyfully to Jerusalem, where they continued to praise and bless God.

"The Head that once was crowned
    with thorns
Is crowned with glory now."

THE ASCENSION

While he blessed them, he was parted
from them, and carried up into heaven.

—*Luke 24:51.*

THE GOOD SHEPHERD ෨ ෨ ෨ ෨

THE story of the shepherd and his sheep is one of the most beloved of all the parables, and through the centuries it has been the inspiration of hymn writers, poets, and artists.

When Jesus told the Parable of the Good Shepherd to His listeners, He knew that the people would well understand the point He was trying to impress on them. They were familiar with sheepherding and sheepfolds, for the sheep used in the Temple sacrifices grazed on the hills of Judea near Jerusalem.

The good shepherd was one who would risk his own life for his sheep. He would save them from the attacks of wild animals and would search for his sheep when they strayed from the fold.

In the eighteenth chapter of Matthew is told the story of the man who had a hundred sheep, of which one was lost. The shepherd left the ninety and nine of his flock and went out into the mountains to seek the sheep that was lost.

If the shepherd were fortunate enough to find the sheep that had strayed, he would rejoice more over finding that one than he would over the "ninety and nine which went not astray."

Jesus is often referred to as "the Good Shepherd." This symbol is based on our Lord's own words in John 10:11: "I am the good shepherd: the good shepherd giveth his life for the sheep."

Here Christ is portrayed as the Good Shepherd, bringing back the lamb that had strayed from the flock. The lamb rests securely in Jesus' arm, while the other sheep gather close to the Master's body.

In His left arm the Master carries a shepherd's crook, the symbol of leadership and protection. In the distance the storm clouds of trouble are dispersing; and the rainbow, a symbol of God's covenant with man, arches across the glowing sky.

In the figure of Jesus, the artist has indicated great strength, thus setting forth the teaching that our Lord is able to defend His lambs, or His children, against the wild beasts that seek to hurt them.

From the original painting in the George Washington Memorial Park, Inc., Whitemarsh, Pennsylvania.

THE GOOD SHEPHERD

I am the good shepherd: the good shepherd giveth his life for the sheep.

—John 10:11.

THE LONELY CHRIST ❦ ❦ ❦ ❦ ❦

THIS painting of Christ standing alone on the hill-top provides a fitting scene for the end of THE WAY, THE TRUTH, AND THE LIFE. It represents the closing moments of a very eventful day in the life of our Lord. Earlier in the day Jesus had ridden triumphantly into Jerusalem amid throngs of people who waved palm branches in His path. He had that day been proclaimed "Jesus the prophet of Nazareth of Galilee."

Later in the day He had cleansed the Temple and had driven out the moneychangers. Then the lame and the blind had pressed about Him and He had healed them.

It was an exciting day, and Jesus was tired, so when eventide was come He went out of the city, probably to Bethany.

We do not know where Jesus lodged that last night, but tradition presumes it may have been at the home of Mary and Martha, whose brother Jesus had raised from the dead.

Neither are we told whether the Saviour spoke to anyone during the closing moments of His life, but we can imagine His message might have well been clothed in the beautiful words of John 14:27: "Peace I leave with you, my peace I give unto you."

Alone, and yet not alone because God was with Him, He stands, clad in pure white raiment, below the towering branches of a palm tree. A broken palm branch trails from His hand. Nearby a little donkey, the burden-bearer of the Bible, grazes in peace and contentment.

Palm branches were used by the Jews as a symbol of spiritual victory, and in Rev. 7:9 we read that the glorified of all nations "stood before the throne and before the Lamb, clothed with white robes, and palms in their hands."

In like manner the Saviour stands, ready to face the sufferings of Crucifixion and death. The long-expected Messiah waits—a lonely Christ indeed!

THE LONELY CHRIST

And he left them, and went out of the city.

—*Matt. 21:17*.